THE
INNER PATH

*Calmness, Compassion & Conversation
in Turbulent Times*

THE
INNER PATH

*Calmness, Compassion & Conversation
in Turbulent Times*

RON ADAMS

Mission Point Press
Traverse City, Michigan

For more resources, visit RonAdamsAuthor.com

Readers are encouraged to go to MissionPointPress.com to contact the author or to find information on how to buy this book in bulk at a discounted rate.

Book design by Angela Saxon
Edited by Tanya Muzumdar
Cover photo by Ron Adams, taken in Steamboat Springs, CO

Published by Mission Point Press
2554 Chandler Rd.
Traverse City, MI 49696
(231) 421-9513
MissionPointPress.com

ISBN: 978-1-954-78626-4

Library of Congress Control Number: 2021909445

Printed in the United States of America

To the late Rev. James A. Adams who passed on to me
the passion for reading and who demonstrated
how to love ordinary people who were in his care.

CONTENTS

TRAILHEAD FOR
THE INNER PATH

"IF"

If you read fast,
The angels of anxiety and hubris may linger.
If you read slowly,
The angel of knowledge may pay you a visit.
If you read thoughtfully,
The angel of growth will arrive.
If you read with an open heart,
The angel of peace will be present.

INTRODUCTION

The only journey is the one within.
Attributed to Rainer Maria Rilke

The pilgrim had been navigating the Via Francigena for several weeks. As he approached the midpoint in the journey, at the top of a mountain range that runs between France and Italy, he was suffering as he limped along. When he stopped and removed his shoes and socks, his bloodied and blistered feet were screaming at him to stop. He tried to continue his journey, but the pain grew so serious that he asked himself, "Why am I doing this?"

Many pilgrims and travelers ask the same question at this stage along the thousand-mile trail. He decided that he would have to find a rental car to take him along the next leg of the journey. He knew he just could not walk for a few days. The rules for a pure, modern pilgrimage stipulate that one may ride when necessary, as long as one doesn't leave the ground, so he could accept assistance. He needed to heal his tired body. The journey had been planned to care for his tired soul.

This is a modern story. Tim had taken a sabbatical from his work in Seattle to make this long-anticipated pilgrimage from Canterbury, in the south of England, to Rome, Italy's eternal city. Many roads and pathways in Europe have religious stories to tell, the Via Francigena among them. Across centuries, millions have traveled the same ancient trail Tim followed, winding through sites of great religious significance, particularly within Christian history.

A pilgrimage is a journey to a shrine or location of moral, historical, or spiritual significance, often proceeding into a faraway place. Along the way, pilgrims search for new meaning and insight about themselves, about others, about nature, or a higher power. These journeys can lead to a dramatic personal transformation. For Tim, his pilgrimage was a quest to come to grips with his religious beliefs—and his doubts. He believed he needed to settle questions that had plagued him for years, and he felt now was the time. He wrote the account of his journey in his powerful memoir, *A Pilgrimage to Eternity*. Other pilgrims seek answers to different questions, and those questions drive them to walk that same path or similar paths around the world. India, soon to be the most populated country in the world, has a rich history of pilgrimage. It is a regular feature of the lives of Indians to travel and take pilgrimage to the many ancient sacred sites around that country. While visiting India a few years ago, I observed pilgrimage all over the country. Some individuals were alone and others with entire families or other social groups who would approach the sacred sites dressed in special outfits for the occasion and offer food and cash gifts along with prayers. Two of the most impressive displays of pilgrimage were seen at the Taj Mahal in Agra and the Ganges River in Varanasi.

Along the pilgrim way, whether it be the Via Francigena (Via) or any number of other trails, the pilgrim seeks a quality that some spiritual masters call "thin places" or liminal space where the spiritual side of life seems to link up with the secular side of life and travelers experience special energy and greater depth of insight. The Via meanders through villages and cities where famous people from the past lived, worked, and died. Mystics like Julian of Norwich and historic figures like Thomas Becket, Augustine, and Joan of Arc, as well as others familiar and unfamiliar, all have special and illuminating life stories that reward the pilgrim. These people left a legacy of creative thoughts to contemplate, inspiration to lift our spirits, and fascinating as well as tragic life stories that can help us navigate our future. We can use these road maps and markers to guide us on our journey.

This book is about journeys and paths that lead to explorations of the heart. Our goal is to create our own healing and calming force in an increasingly turbulent world. Most of us will not be able to walk the ancient pilgrim pathways of the Old World, but we can launch a journey right where we are, one that will benefit us as we engage with this complicated and often chaotic new world. When we travel without a direction, we meander through life rather than intentionally setting out on an inward journey. The meandering approach to life does not offer a sense of peace or sure footing during times of great uncertainty. Simply meandering does not give us the inner resilience needed for this time of worldwide pandemic, social unrest, and cultural upheavals.

Too often, our culture considers life an athletic contest, with winners and losers locked in combat. Our culture tells us that only the strong will survive and that aggressive action is the only way to engage with others. Standing up for your cause with every personal resource you have is regarded as the antidote to suffering. But seldom does an aggressive stance lead to inward peace, nor does it solve the intractable problems we face. We are left wondering whether we can find a better way.

We can!

The Path is a seven-step intentional and modern journey that prepares us for a calm, clear, purposeful way of living, one that will uplift and sustain us during these chaotic, turbulent, and distressing times. Our aim is not merely to calm, however. We can achieve and maintain a peaceful interior life, no matter what our circumstances—if we follow the seven steps described in parts one and two and the steps in part three. Together, we'll prepare for our journey, study the road map outlined here, and explore a new path on our journey through life.

This journey draws on ancient spiritual practices, as well as modern practices with traditional religious language stripped away. The road map is intended for people of all faiths, as well as those who don't adhere to any faith tradition. The practices also apply to other spheres of life, from politics to social activism, from personal to business relationships, and from our homes out into the world.

What is it that prepares me to write this book? My academic background was in theology/philosophy with over one hundred hours of post graduate education. Following that time of study, I embarked on what turned out to be three distinct career paths, each about twelve years in duration. The common denominator between them was my intense interest in observing people and culture. I was first a clergyman, then a small business owner, and, finally, enjoyed a career in information technology client relations. All three periods of my adult life have given me opportunities to study people and culture. It is from that rich soil of observation and research that I have come to the belief that this kind of path of interior development is critical for our culture.

I wrote this section as the COVID-19 pandemic gripped the globe. Chronic anxiety has enveloped most of the world as our normal ways of working, playing, relaxing, entertaining, educating, and caring for others are all disrupted. Countless millions around the world are out of work and out of school, worried about paying bills, worried about their own and their family's healthcare, worried about the future. Millions are in danger of losing their homes and the means to provide for their families. Now that the vaccine program is underway around the world, new hope is arising, although our normal ways of going about daily life seem to be permanently altered, and there is much grief over those lost to COVID-19.

In normal times, many of us ignore the reality of death for ourselves and our family, but the pandemic has brought death to the forefront of our attention. Every day, news programs tally the numbers of COVID-19 related deaths. Until now, many of our fellow citizens lived their lives as if death only happens to others, not themselves, but we have begun to see death coming closer—and that is a terrifying reality to many of us.

Alain de Botton, a well-regarded French philosopher, addressed the stark reality of so much death in a *New York Times* feature on March 22, 2020, soon after COVID-19 struck America in earnest. In plain-spoken language he stated a "perpetual" rule: "All human beings are vulnerable to being randomly exterminated at any time, by a virus, an accident, or the actions of our fellow man.... Suffering is randomly distributed, it makes no sense, it is simply absurd." But then Alain reminds readers of a positive lesson attributed to the twentieth-century author/philosopher Albert Camus: "We need to love our fellow damned humans and work …for the amelioration of suffering."

The world suffers as COVID-19 wreaks havoc on random lives at a terrifying pace. But at the same time, mankind is facing other equally serious crises around the globe: catastrophic environmental threats; additional health concerns; ethnic and racial injustices; as well as serious global financial challenges. Other crises are more personal: the gap between the haves and have-nots is huge and growing; too many people lack healthy communication skills; and pop culture defines success and happiness by the amount of wealth we accumulate. As the January 6, 2021, storming of the Capitol vividly demonstrated, we have deep and often violent tendencies when frustrated by political differences.

How can we make sense of all this trauma and tragedy? Is there hope for us in our suffering? Circumstances and existential questions are forcing us all to think about our place in the world. We need to explore deeper matters and ask more probing questions. A closer look or reflection about our current culture will make my point clearly. Only a thoughtful inward journey, a pilgrimage that calms the soul, will prepare us for the tough times we are enduring and the uncertain times ahead. If you feel anxious, confused, restless, lost, or gridlocked within the world right now, it's time for a pilgrimage of your own.

The Path offers a journey to calmness, which leads to clear and deliberate intentions as we walk through these and other crises in a way that gives our lives deeper meaning and purpose.

The journey mapped out in these pages prepares you for your own unique journey. Any journey, whether religious, humanistic, political, or as a social activist, requires well-considered preparations, to ensure we are adequately equipped for the task. These preparations make us balanced and compassionate, as we embrace our various causes.

The quest takes place in a seven-step journey I call The Path. The first section of the journey, Being, requires four interrelated steps, each a deepening of the previous one. Step one, Focus, introduces the practice of meditation. Step two, Relax, builds and deepens on the idea of meditation as we learn to slow and quiet our minds. Step three, Study, continues the deepening process, with intentional reading and listening to some of the finest resources at our disposal. And step four, Reflect, promotes the exploration of the first three steps, inviting you to sit back and let your mind wander among all the new ideas you will experience and learn. An exciting thing happens along the way—new ideas and thoughts begin to form, and some of them are little glimpses of possibility that never occurred to you before. These are what I refer to as "aha moments" of the soul. We aim to become more fully alive human beings as we walk along our interior pathway on our physical journey through life.

The second section of The Path consists of Doing. It focuses on the three final steps of The Path: Discard, Give, and Act. We cannot succeed at whatever we want to do well if we have not first become a fully alive and balanced person in our interior life. Many wise people have observed that going into the battle of life without developing the practices of Being will result in ineffective Doing. Step five, Discard, explores the power of cleaning out the negative messages and practices in our past, starting with an examination of our shadow side—trash—in all its forms. Step six, Give, discusses all the ways we can give of ourselves to strangers, to friends, and to the world. Finally, step seven, Act, examines thoughtful compassion and social justice activism.

Once we have walked along The Path into a calm approach toward life and a deepening understanding of how to engage with the world in compassion and activism, we are ready for the next important practice, that of improving our ability to converse. The third section of this book explores the urgent need for better conversation that helps us cross the many ideologies of politics and religion that we find ourselves either arguing or ignoring. After all, The Path is about engaging in rational discussion, rather than pushing to win an argument. This provides new and value-based solutions that materialize when individuals representing two sides of an argument learn to listen and communicate more effectively. Our goal is to open doors to meaningful, life-changing conversations with people representing all the many polarities dividing our nation and our world. Ideally, The Path transcends our ideology, providing new helpful approaches for conversing with individuals on opposite sides of any issue. Democrats and Republicans, Christians and secular humanists, liberals and conservatives, wealthy and disadvantaged, members of different cultural traditions—all can prepare for their unique and individual pathways joining us on this journey toward calm. This section offers six ways to foster empathic skills that can help us to converse with people of all backgrounds.

So now, let's walk together as I outline the terrain of a seven-step path that leads to a calmness of spirit and an ability to speak respectfully and productively with one another. You may want to read a chapter a day and let its message resonate before proceeding to the next chapter and next step. This method of reading fits well with ancient practices of reading and reflecting.

May you travel peacefully into the interior of your life!

PART ONE

BEING –
The Path Toward
Calmness

FOCUS: MEDITATION

Mindfulness isn't difficult,
we just need to remember to do it.
Sharon Salzberg

Meditation is a way of reducing
resistance to the reality of our lives.

Tara Brach

The Cenacle Retreat House on the north side of Chicago is a respite from the crazy, busy streets just outside its doors. I approached this retreat center with trepidation welling up within me. My friend, Matt, and I were about to embark on a weekend silent retreat. I had never been silent for a day, let alone three days! It turned out to be a pivotal event in my spiritual development. No longer could meditation be primarily an academic exercise. When I immersed myself in contemplative silence and reflection, I began to feel my body and mind relax. It wasn't easy to keep silent at times when I was used to conversing, particularly during meals. But the training of my mind and the instruction we received from the leaders was helpful in terms of how to view my place in the big scheme of things. My appreciation for the work that many monks have done over the centuries grew immensely. A silent retreat helps break the habits we form while rushing through life without interior strength-building.

I use the modern word *focus* to highlight the ancient practice that was, and is, meditation. This practice has to be the first of the seven practices I am recommending. Everything good flows from meditation. It serves as the cornerstone for a successful journey throughout life. If we don't focus our minds through meditation first, then the effectiveness and benefit of the other practices are called into question. And for the religious as well, some modern forms of prayer incorporate aspects of meditation. In her book, *Spiritual Rebel*, Sarah Bowen writes: "We already possess an inner knowing of who we are and of God. The key is in direct experience (through meditation) rather than the learning of beliefs." This inner knowledge speaks to us all, whether we are believers who follow religious traditions, or whether we are humanists. For my purposes in this book, humanism refers to a range of beliefs that are at least agnostic about the existence of a God. Many humanists believe we are responsible for our own moral code and our search for happiness in this life. I've also heard quasi-religious folks who love environmentalism and social justice refer to themselves as humanists. This category, like many today, is somewhat fluid, reflecting the postmodern age in which we live.

Meditation is the beginning of an interior journey that can result in calmness in the midst of a turbulent world. When the news media is constantly bombarding us with negative images and stories from around the world, when corporations are demanding more and more productivity per day and then abandoning their workers seemingly at whim, when our children's future success seems to be dependent on having parents fully engaged in all activities to the point of exhaustion, the power of meditation becomes critically important to our mental and physical health. Medical studies have shown that meditation and other calming activities can lower blood pressure and lessen anxiety levels.

The first step on The Path is to incorporate a practice of meditation and contemplation. Many aspire to achieve the practical side of meditation and mindfulness. Perhaps they wish to get some relief from the mental drudgery they find in their work. Or their lives are so hectic they have no "me time." Zen master Thich Nhat Hanh has pointed out, "The feeling that any task is a nuisance will soon disappear if it is done in mindfulness."

The world is not only suffering from the COVID-19 pandemic, but also witnessing protest movements that call our attention to systemic racism in our police forces, in our society, and around the globe. Anxiety among the population is soaring, whether we are engaged in protest or not. Recently I came across an important resource from the website Ten Percent Weekly. In "What the Pandemic Can Teach Us," American Buddhist monk and teacher, Pema Chodron, offers thoughtful instructions on how to meditate in ways that begin to help us deal with this onslaught of problems. Her words don't solve the problems around us, but they offer us comfort and a realistic assessment:

> If I had to make a prediction, I would say that things will get more polarized, that people will either become more fundamentalist or

more open-hearted.... One's fear grows rather than diminishes and one's sense of danger grows rather than lessening. Whereas if you're opening more and more, you feel more and more comfortable with uncertainty, more comfortable with what life is presenting to you, or at least more flexible or ready to work with whatever might come.

Some of us shy away from meditation because it takes discipline to practice on a regular basis. Some of us have never quieted our minds long enough to meditate. And many don't understand how meditation could possibly be beneficial. But throughout the centuries and millennia, the ancient sages and pilgrims learned and chronicled their experiences on the avenue to peaceful, contemplative living—and now scientists and practitioners are confirming the ancient wisdom and the modern health benefits that result from meditation—peace and healthy living.

Without meditation, we live lives of random actions and reactions. Some Buddhists call our brain "the monkey mind," since it jumps from one subject to another like a young monkey bounding from branch to branch. When I was a child growing up in Iowa, my parents took us back to their small city of origin, Richmond, Indiana, each summer. The one thing we always wanted to do after that long trek along the two-lane route from Iowa to Indiana pre-interstate days was visit Glenn Miller Park. Right in the middle of the city, we could drive along curving roads that wind through the wooded hillsides and past gurgling streams. But that wasn't the only treat; the best stop of all was the monkey exhibit that the park maintained for many years. We watched as monkeys ran and jumped from ropes to branches to hanging tires to the fencing that surrounded the place around and above. The young ones frolicked with each other and pestered the older ones. The older monkeys eventually tired of the antics and chased the youngsters, squawking loudly. We watched, fascinated, as the monkeys ate their bananas and veggies and picked fleas or bugs off each other's fur. It appeared to us as if they ate them! That, of course, grossed us out in a childish and funny way. Sometimes the monkeys sat and stared at us as we stared at them. At other times they slept and paid no attention to us. The monkeys were unpredictable, always changing their activities from one moment to the next. Their monkey brains were hard at work, filling their days with random activities.

The uncontrolled monkey mind in our own brain shares the same characteristic. We may start out thinking about what we have to do today, and then suddenly remember a piece of gossip we heard yesterday, and we add our own interpretation and judgment. We frequently review events from our past that make us feel badly. Dark thoughts may flitter across the screen of our mind. Then, the very next moment, we may be thinking altruistic thoughts, and our mind proceeds to a Walter Mitty-type fantasy we enjoy tremendously. Seemingly, we don't have much control over this part of our thoughts.

Each day the story replays itself in an endless loop, almost like a stream-of-consciousness film. However, meditation teaches us to observe this happening and take a respite from it. We do that by focusing on our breathing, or counting, or enumerating our blessings. At first, the practice only distracts our monkey mind for a few seconds, and then we find ourselves back in the mind movie—the monkey brain. When that happens, meditation teachers remind us to return to our focus, without judging ourselves or feeling like failures. Over time, if we stick with meditation for a reasonable number of days, we will notice subtle changes in our ability to concentrate.

A favorite author of mine, Stephen Batchelor, says that the goal of meditation is "non-reactive stillness." Over time, meditation will begin to help us with our reactions to the events and conversations of life. We will become thoughtful instead of reactive, even in moments when something surprises us. It won't be perfection, of course, but it will move in the direction of thoughtfulness or mindfulness. This is the goal of step one.

Meditative acts include contemplation, deep thought, musing, pondering, focused thoughts, and thoughtful and calming writing. Practitioners often teach one of many forms, such as mindfulness, focused meditation, walking meditation, mantra meditation, and transcendental meditation. Every teacher has favorite ways to think about the practice and the key to remember is that there is no one correct way.

Filmmaker David Lynch wrote an article on meditation in which he states: "I heard a phrase, 'True happiness is not out there. It lies within.'... This phrase had a ring of truth.... One day it hit me that meditation would be the way to go within."

Many people discover that meditating first thing in the morning is the best way to start their day and the most beneficial use of meditation. Start small and simple, but the practice can get as complicated as you like, especially if you follow Buddhist techniques that have been perfecting meditation models for centuries. By small and simple, I mean that when you begin your practice, you can devote as few as ten minutes a day to meditation. Remember—there is no one single correct way to meditate. Any intention you follow will get you started just fine.

Buddhist monk Thich Nhat Hanh is one of many who suggest you focus on your breath, concentrating on exhaling and inhaling alone. "Breathe in and breathe out," he advises. In this form of meditation, you can calm and quiet your mind. This isn't easy! As you will discover, it requires surprisingly hard work. Our minds have wills of their own, and they aren't easily controlled.

But you might choose among many other ways to meditate. You can calmly review the workings of different parts of your body, or you can assess your energy. You can choose to list all the things that make you grateful. You can count to one hundred forwards and backwards. Some focus on what they can do for others or what others have done for them. You might repeat a mantra, reflect on the day, reflect on the past week, ponder an inspirational quote, evaluate what makes you feel fulfilled. Or you might want to start with a guided meditation.

Guided meditations can be found on many online websites, led by recognized meditation gurus like Sharon Salzberg, Ram Dass, Tara Brach, and others. Choose a subject that interests you and then just relax and listen while the guide tells you exactly how to breathe and what to do for the session. You will often hear them remind you to "soften your belly." They want you to be as relaxed as possible. Then they will suggest thoughts involving the subject you've chosen.

I like to think of mindfulness as the all-day practice of meditation. It encapsulates the idea of being on a journey that brings meaning into our lives. The West has brought this Eastern practice of meditation, and now mindfulness, into common usage, recognizing that it offers a plethora of applications in the business world, education, and healthcare, as well as the spiritual realm. Even professional athletes are discovering the benefits of taking slow and deep breaths as a way to calm themselves and allow their bodies to focus more intently.

Recently I had the privilege of watching my three-year-old grandson Xavier play in his room. He focused for a few seconds on one object and then quickly jumped to the next activity. At most, he kept his attention on a favorite activity for five minutes. He came back to it, but you could see as he made his way around the room that his eyes landed on something else and that would trigger a new interest, maybe for just a few seconds. Now that Xavier is beginning his fourth year, he is already learning to focus on his favorite activity: indoor volleyball. We use a balloon as a volleyball. After watching his parents play sand volleyball, he knows how to pretend to send the signals to us, his partners, before serving the ball across the beanbag chair in the living room. As children grow older, if they have good training from loving caretakers, they learn to control and then to focus on a task, a necessary skill that allows them to function and successfully complete those tasks throughout life.

When I was a child living in Iowa, meditation was not part of our lingo. And it certainly was not part of our religious life; prayer meant something altogether different. Now after six decades of cultural immersion, meditation's evolution into Western styles has taken place. Even some conservative religious traditions now consider meditation acceptable as another aspect of prayer. If this could be accomplished in sixty years, imagine the evolution of customs and practices over several thousands—or millions—of years.

Westerners now recognize great benefits stemming from incorporating meditation into their religious practices. Thoughtful Christians have distinguished the differences between traditional forms of prayer and the more modern and helpful practice of Christian-oriented meditation. Traditionally, prayer falls into several forms. In a form of prayer, supplication, Christians ask their God for help with tasks or concerns. Intercessory prayer is a deep, emotional prayer in which devout Christians intercede with God on behalf of another person. Contemplative, or "centering," prayer is much like meditation. And gratitude is a fourth way many Christians direct their prayers.

In the past, most churches did not explore contemplative prayer; they focused particularly on intercession and supplication as genres of prayer. This was a result of most training programs for ministers focusing on theological dogma, church administration, and evangelism rather than a more expansive study of the wisdom and spiritual literature from around the world. When the Eastern influence began spreading in the latter part of the twentieth century, many embraced meditation because it filled an unmet need. Until recently, only the monastic community engaged in these practices, and the average person in the congregation did not have training in meditation, this much-needed form of contemplation. That is no longer the case. Meditation, for the most part, is still an individual practice rather than a corporate practice, but at least the clergy are open to these new practices among their laity.

Many churches find it challenging to incorporate contemplative prayer into their public programming or liturgy. Nevertheless, there is a growing recognition among some leaders that we must recapture a balance between the inner life of devotion and the outer life of service and activism. In fact, it is the inner life that provides the foundation, the proper approach, and the strength to engage in the life of service and action. It makes a huge difference for those leaders who recognize these differences. Conservative Christians are realizing that adopting a meditation practice or a contemplative prayer practice does not diminish their love of belief-oriented faith, and over time it may improve their ability to have conversations across barriers of religious belief and cultural difference. Liberal Christians who feel a real passion for social justice initiatives can discover that incorporating meditation as a foundational part of their journey will augment their social justice actions. It will cause them to be less abrasive and reactive and more compassionate in this important work. And for the humanists who want to develop a secular spirituality in their practices, meditation is very useful. It helps lessen the tendency toward harshness and judgmental attitudes. One of my treasured books was written by an unknown fourteenth-century mystic, titled *The Cloud of Unknowing*. The author speaks of the Christian contemplative practices. Even though I was raised in a devout Christian home, I never heard of these meditative practices until I was an adult. It was just not part of our tradition.

I am not suggesting that only one way leads to a deeper and more thoughtful life. What I am suggesting is that interior journeys reap benefits that have been passed down to us from antiquity. The practices have survived because of their meaningful rewards. They work to calm individuals by helping them get through rough days. In my estimation, meditation practices are preparation for whatever perspectives, worldviews, or identities we are living into. Intense practitioners of Buddhist meditation encounter very esoteric teachings which are all well and good, but the American audience who may encounter meditation in a Christian or other humanist setting just needs simple, modern wording and explanation to help them relax and gain the benefit of their practice. If that continues to happen, as it seems to be, then we will significantly improve our ability to speak with one another across boundaries that currently separate us. Meditation is the engine that propels us along our pathways, softening our quick reactions and opening our hearts to new possibilities.

The late Stephen Levine wrote a fascinating book entitled *A Year to Live*, in which he challenged his readers to spend one year living as if they only had that year to live. He outlined practices to help us dive deeply into a commitment to make our daily lives more meaningful. The chapter "A Commitment to Life" discusses the changes practitioners observe as they meditate: "We begin to live our life firsthand, tasting our food instead of thinking it, listening to the music instead of just humming it, seeing a new face without characterizing it, lovemaking as if it were the first time. We break the dreamlike quality of a half-attended life."

He says that our minds often get foggy with our own judgments and confusion or arguments. We need to simply note it, be aware of it, and let it pass through our awareness without judgment. As we become more experienced, this practice of awakening can become part of our daily routine, according to Levine. His advice:

> Establish a daily practice of awakening. There are many remarkable psychological processes and therapies, but nothing will do for you what a meditation practice can. No other healing will reach quite so deeply. When the mind has softened its belly and let go of the hardness that obscures our inherent clarity, our senses open in a most gratifying manner. We can hear more subtly, see more detail, and thought becomes more lucid and distinct as our feelings are experienced floating in an expanding awareness. We settle into a moment-to-moment mindfulness of the changing sensations within each breath, watching thoughts arise and disappear, letting go of all that obstructs the vastness of our birthright. Approaching our true nature, like a pilgrim weary from the long journey who can at last put aside his pack, we rest in being.

STEP ONE ACTION PLAN

Begin a practice of daily meditation by choosing a time of day and location that is comfortable for you. Invite a friend to join you or simply practice on your own. Exploring an online resource for guided meditation may be helpful to get started. One of my friends has begun to ask "Alexa," the online assistant sold by Amazon, to give him a guided meditation. How modern is that! Enjoy the journey!

THE PATH STEP TWO
RELAX: SLOW AND QUIET

*I don't believe that ideas originate within me
But rather, if I do the deep work of creating space
By getting out of the way and quieting my mind,
Sometimes on those rare and remarkable days,
They arrive and pay me a visit.*

Day Schildkret

My wife, Melinda, and I were visiting Vietnam and had the privilege of staying with her nephew, a pilot for one of the Vietnamese airlines. He flies the big jets in that part of the world. Living in the bustling metropolis, Ho Chi Minh City (formerly Saigon), is an experience different from residing in any American city. An estimated 43 million scooters fill the streets of Vietnam—and we could easily believe that 40 million of those were with us in that city alone. Scooters were everywhere, all around us, as we traveled in Uber-like taxis. Only the most major of intersections had traffic signals. The traffic just flowed along at about 20 to 30 miles per hour without any screeching of tires or honking of horns. When we wanted to cross the street, the method was to carefully, but steadily, just step out into traffic. "Pole pole," our guide said …"just keep walking slowly and the traffic will move around you as you cross the four lanes of the street." My wife's nephew had grown up in Kenya. In the lingua franca, pole pole (po-lay po-lay) in Kiswahili means "slow slow." The Kiswahili phrase is a reminder that other parts of the world recognize the value of slowing down.

The word I use to describe this slowdown process is Relax. Ancient practices promoted—and continue to promote—quieting and slowing of the mind. Nearly every path toward deeper spirituality has stressed the need to slow down and quiet your mind. We cannot possibly be hurried and harried and still reap the benefits of an inward path. Slow and quiet hold the keys to deepening one's interior life. Relax signifies the ancient spiritual practice passed down to us from monks and sages. We find it nearly impossible to hear the small, quiet observations of our mind if we are rushing about, always feeling the pressure to do more or pack more into the day.

Modern-day life often rejects timeless truths. We are being pushed to be more productive and more efficient. We are being told to do, do, and do more in order to stay ahead of the pack. Moms and dads shuffle kids from one activity to the next in hopes that they will stay ahead or at least stay with their peers. Maybe they will even develop an advantage in an increasingly competitive world. They are operating from a middle-class cultural imperative that suggests that working harder and faster is the only way to achieve. Consequently, parents are exhausted, and their kids are feeling levels of anxiety they should not have to feel.

In her book, *Spiritual Rebel,* Sarah Bowen captures the modern condition when she recalls,

> Over the next ten years my apartments and jobs improved. Traveling extensively on business and vacationing in foreign countries, my passport proved I could get around. Stockpiling stuff, chasing success, and wooing money, everything appeared to be going as planned. Yet I was drowning in addiction, and a fathomless void was growing inside.

We don't have to be a world traveler to have this experience of being harried. Observe many young parents or professionals today and you will see the frenetic pace that is gnawing away at their chance to have peace and contentment. This approach is damaging their souls.

COVID-19, twenty-four-hour news feeds, environmental concerns, systemic racism, peaceful protests, violence, wildfires, devastating hurricanes, nationalist movements, job and economic concerns, unemployment figures, nonstop political drama, school and business closings, and lockdowns are just some of the anxiety-producing threats. Our current condition is calling us to slow down? The list of anxiety-producing threats is getting longer. The temptation is to react by speeding up our responses in a futile attempt to control the uncontrollable. But, actually, the reverse is the solution. If we meditate and slow down, we stand a much better chance of calming ourselves, considering deeply, and responding in a wise, reasonable way to any conflict we confront.

A case can be made that if we do not see a slowing of reactivity and an appreciation for quiet times after a month or so of meditation, then perhaps something isn't working correctly. If you continue your budding meditative practice, you should experience some life-enhancing changes that will begin in small increments.

Some social scientists have made the case that many problems have been tolerated and even instigated by the smartest and most powerful people of our age. In fact, one theory of the future holds that the more intelligent a civilization becomes, the less able it will be to survive the future. This theory posits that more intelligence produces more inventions which lead to greater population growth, which in turn increasingly depletes natural resources. Eventually the society collapses—or so the theory goes. Insects can survive anything, but it is increasingly questionable if intelligent life has the capacity to change the trajectory on which it is traveling.

So what is the path forward if we want a less anxious existence in an uncertain future? Those who observe this situation from a spiritual or well-being perspective believe the answer must be internal. Interior growth does not diminish the value of solutions offered by science. It just realizes that science is not enough. By developing our inner strength, we create a life that reduces anxiety even in chaotic times.

Relax, the second step in The Path, goes hand in hand with the practice of meditation we discussed in step one. In fact, relaxation is a deepening of that practice. We think of meditation happening at a specific time, but relaxing is a practice that can occur any hour of the day. Relaxing will help usher in the ability to begin to slow ourselves down and quiet our anxious minds, and lead to calm and peace even in the midst of chaos. The COVID-19 pandemic and the resulting self-isolation have inspired helpful resources. Professional counselors are keeping busy with the increasing turbulence being felt by their clients, and Internet sites like Calm, Headspace, and Ten Percent Happier are helping individuals deal with the anxiety-inciting world.

One good practice that helps us relax is very easily accomplished through a breathing exercise that can be done at any time of day, at home, or in a crowd. All you do is take a slow and long breath in, hesitate for two full seconds at the top of the breath and then slowly exhale. The entire exercise should take about fifteen to twenty seconds. Just focusing on that allows our spirit to relax and rest.

Another useful idea to help us slow down, and consequently relax, is to intentionally drive slower when out and about. The second important part of this is to turn off the radio while driving around town. A few moments without music or news will help us lessen the ambient chatter that seems to always be in the background. Another idea to help us slow down is to turn our devices off for an hour or so at particular times of the day. This will help train our minds to relax instead of always subconsciously listening for the next beep signifying an email, text, calendar reminder, or news item coming into our device. Slow, quiet, and peaceful thoughts will help interrupt the barrage of bad news from around the world.

Author Day Schildkret speaks of slowing down in his book *Morning Altars*. He compares a slower, more deliberate life to "a well-cooked stew that finds its flavor over time." He adds, "Attention deficit is not unusual for anyone who is plugged in to the modern media circus, like the attention draining, Facebooklandia. We have become a culture of distraction, unable or unwilling to be here because there's always the next thing to consume."

Like Schildkret, we all have observed clusters of people, even families gathered in restaurants, who are close physically, but distant emotionally. They ignore each other as they concentrate on communicating through their cell phones. "Always hungry for the new and the next, we have become a people who do not know how to be here," Schildkret notes. His remedy is to "do the deep work of creating space by getting out of the way and quieting my mind." We can all benefit from that approach.

All this said, does that mean quickness and rushing should never be part of our lives? No. When my late-arriving plane landed in Phoenix recently, I knew my connecting flight was already boarding. I politely, but firmly hurried into the crowded aisle and asked to be allowed to jump ahead of others to get to my connecting flight as quickly as possible. I sprinted to the gate and arrived just in time, the last person to board. When I'm playing the popular game of pickleball, which is like tennis on a smaller scale, I am ready to smash a high return into my opponent's court with all the force I can muster in order to win the point. The Path does not stop me from energetically participating in the fun things that I enjoy. The interior path is much deeper than a sport, and it is not diminished by my rush to catch the next flight. As Madisyn Taylor, an online writer, reminds us, "A life savored slowly need not be passive, inefficient, or slothful."

The telephone message on the phone of Baelyn Elspeth, a tea ceremony expert, is highly revealing and inspiring:

> Thank you so much for taking the time to connect, I may be serving tea, on retreat, off in the forest, or on the other side of the world. Due to this flow of life and my continued desire to remain present unto it, it may take some time to receive a response. I will only be responding to those messages that require my direct attention so as to minimize my time exchanged with technology.

The ancient practice known as the tea ceremony is all about relaxation, quiet, and deliberate communal sharing in the preparation and serving of the tea. It is the essence of mindfulness. The message on Baelyn's phone reminds us of all the other wonderful possibilities the world offers us.

Baelyn is obviously not enamored by the intrusiveness of technology. She has figured out how to disconnect when she needs to, allowing nothing to interfere with her interior journey of meditative slowness and quiescence on the way to peace. We can choose among many ways to do this.

For instance, a few months ago, I visited a retreat center in a southern Michigan forest. The entrance was a rather long gravel road through overhanging trees. A rough wooden sign hung on one of the trees. It read: "Begin to Slow Down." That is precisely the advice I needed in order to enter the retreat in the correct frame of mind. What would our days look like if we used that as our reminder when life overwhelms us and our schedules haunt us? We would certainly have the perspective and thoughtfulness to respond more effectively.

In a wooded setting like the retreat center I visited, a favorite technique is to do walking meditation. Just walk very slowly through the pathways in the woods with a very soft and subtle mind. This should be the opposite of the fast walking that we do when we are wanting to work out and stretch our muscles. This is all about mindfulness as we walk. Our minds can just drink in the sights and sounds. When we walk at a slow pace, the senses become more alive, and our spirit can more easily become one with nature. It is very soothing. How is this different from meditation? The meditation I speak of in this book is a specific action we take at a particular time of day in order to calm our mind. The relaxation or slowing down of life that I'm referencing in this chapter is more the awareness that all of life needs to take a relaxing break, a more mindful approach to each moment of the day. It complements the meditation practice we engage in.

~

STEP TWO ACTION PLAN

Begin to practice slow and quiet at multiple intervals throughout the day. Deep breathing, a short prayer, reciting a mantra, or simply closing your eyes and willing your mind to empty will prepare you to engage with life in a much calmer fashion.

Learn to sit with your thoughts at different times during the day. In time you can train your mind to be less distracted by aimless wandering. Eventually you will be able to address big questions you may have avoided. Refrain from rushing on to the next chapter of The Path. Let the thoughts that arise from reading this book just simmer in your mind. Then, only when you are ready, when you believe you have understood the messages, move on to the next chapter.

THE PATH STEP THREE
STUDY: READ AND LISTEN

It is often said that the more time one
puts into something, the luckier they get.
Anonymous

The Kingdom of Bhutan is hidden in one of the most remote regions, north and east of India on the Himalayas's eastern edge. Known for its dramatic monasteries, fortresses (dzongs), semitropical vegetation, steep mountains, and deep valleys, this landlocked country shares a border with Tibet. The number of annual visitors to Bhutan is very carefully controlled, to preserve the beauty and integrity of this ancient civilization. The people of Bhutan have chosen to avoid the tendency of other Third World countries to become westernized. Their beloved King Jigme Khesar Namgyel Wangchuck instituted what he calls (in translation) the "Gross National Happiness" index, which should be a model for cultures everywhere.

As a culture, the people decided to reject the capitalist notion that measures success by the Gross National Product. Instead of focusing on the consumption of increasingly more resources, the government of Bhutan aspires to work toward the happiness of each citizen. They emphasize interior happiness rather than happiness gained through acquisition—in sharp contrast to the Western world's addiction to shopping and consuming in a futile search for happiness.

My friends, David and Nancy, visited the remote country of Bhutan. In advance of their trip, they studied the country and carefully planned their route and itinerary. The journey required several stages. Leaving from Michigan, they flew to New York. From New York they endured the extremely long flight to Dubai. From Dubai they flew to New Delhi, where they stayed for three days to see the sights of that tremendous city. From New Delhi they flew to the Kingdom of Bhutan. A long trip, but one they believed would be transformative.

In Bhutan, they toured several areas and eventually made their way to the valley of Paro and the city of the same name. David and Nancy had a destination in mind. They wanted to take a pilgrimage to the famous and very remote monastery called the "Tiger's Nest" (Taktsang), which is precariously situated on the sheer cliffs thousands of feet above the Paro Valley. (You can see photos of this monastery on Instagram using #bhutantigersnest.) The hike to Tiger's Nest Monastery starts at about ten thousand feet and meanders through valleys and uphill treks, through forested areas and sheer cliff exposures. The final leg of the journey involves more than seven hundred steps to reach the monastery.

For many, this quest offers an intense spiritual experience. David, age 72 at the time, always relishes a physical challenge. In recounting the excursion, he told me he found himself determined to ascend the trail faster than anyone else in his group. After his trip, he reported that he felt a distinct spiritual experience when he reached the extraordinary mountain cliff where Tiger's Nest perches. As he rested and looked over the valley far below, he marveled at the scenery surrounding the monastery. "I was moved in a very special way," he said, attributing his reaction to the thrill of the intense journey and then the sight of the mountain valley far below his seat on the cliff. "I recognized within myself a sense that nature is so much bigger and more powerful than I am."

Nancy took the journey more slowly, and said her spiritual experience was based on marveling at the beautiful forested scenery that was unveiled on her way up the mountain. She described the smell of the pine and enjoyment in discovering unusual mountain flowers and plants. She also described the bird calls and the gurgling sounds of the mountain streams as they coursed down to the valley below. Nancy and David experienced a spiritual awakening in the same place, but in two very different ways. We all interact with our environment in unique ways. For both of my friends, the entire experience became a day they will never forget. Their spiritual experience began with advance preparations, by studying, reading, and speaking with others who went before them. Then they invested great attention and effort to prepare for this amazing trip. None of us can expect growth without effort and often the need for study.

Few of us will ever have the opportunity to gaze upon the 23,000-foot-high slopes in the Himalayas. We may not be able to experience firsthand the culture found in the Kingdom of Bhutan. But we can experience great spiritual moments of our own, through meditation, study, and reflection.

The theme of this step on The Path is the value of investing effort into your journey inward. As all athletes know, the more practice and energy they dedicate to their sport, the more accomplished they become. Everyone who invests the necessary time and effort can experience authentic and beautiful spiritual moments wherever they are in life. The depth of the experience depends on the depth of commitment. Like every good thing, commitment to preparation and the effort required to master the subject or undertaking will determine the reward.

Recently when I was looking at my Instagram app, I came across a photographer from Chicago who made this statement: "I prefer the world in my head, where magic exists and time does not." The creator JM has discovered the source that inspires his work. He overturns the common adage that we must get out of our heads and into our bodies if we want to succeed. In his head, he finds inspiration, he finds the essence that makes his life extraordinary.

All of us can do the same thing in our own way, whatever our goal may be. Some of us escape time and place when we read an inspiring biography or a well-crafted novel. Others find inspiration as they stroll through a lush, colorful botanical garden, or when they watch a skilled chef preparing an outstanding meal on a television cooking show. Whatever experiences lead you to inspiration, the point is the same: You cannot traverse The Path very far without exerting some form of effort. Study is the word I am using for this stretch of The Path. The ancient sages valued deep reading, thoughtful questioning, and listening, and we would do well to do the same.

In ancient eras, only a few could read, while the masses were left without education. In our modern era we are unbelievably privileged to have access to the world's information through well-stocked libraries, on the Internet while we sit at home, on our phones, and in books we acquire at bookstores.

My favorite form of study is reading books which discuss the interior evolution of our lives. Close to the top of my list is Thomas Moore's *A Religion of One's Own*. His subtitle reveals the revolutionary ground he is trying to cover: *A Guide to Creating a Personal Spirituality in a Secular World*. I have grown to love this book because it challenges me. He expands my view of the world and suggests new directions for exploring my interior life. Moore has given me several "aha moments of the soul."

In the second sentence of his book, Moore says, "I hold the religious traditions in the highest regard, have always given art a central place in my life, believed in a spiritual existence in a secular world, and find joy in the erotic life." Several pages later, he suggests that "Traditional religion may well need an overhaul from top to bottom" but he adds "personal religion is a requirement. It is the indispensable foundation of an intelligent, open hearted approach to life." And then the book follows the trajectory of his introduction when he says, "The more traditions I study and borrow from, the deeper my spiritual life becomes."

This is a book I've reread several times and have taught to a few small groups. In these pages Moore reveals many diverse ways to approach the spiritual life—through the eyes of purely secular avenues of nature and art, through other religions, and by studying the works of the mystics. He talks about how pleasure, desire, and the deeply sensual can enhance life. He discusses openly how lovemaking with your partner should ideally be a spiritual experience with a depth of meaning that most never attain because our eyes haven't been opened to that possibility.

Let me give you a taste of Moore's wonderful use of language and concepts that may open up new vistas of understanding for you:

> The secular and the spiritual are two sides of a coin. There is no separation between them. If you want to be spiritual, you have to live fully in this world—and vice versa. If you want to be spiritual, you have to live completely in this world of the senses and your ego. You can't be an earthy, sensual, fun-loving person if you don't make peace with the deeper, spiritual questions of humankind. Not only do you have a spiritual practice; that spirituality has a direct impact on all aspects of your life.... Most traditionally religious people start at the wrong end. They begin by addressing the afterlife and miss out on the sacred and the eternal right in front of them.... Art is a good place to taste the eternal, especially if it's presented with suitable mystery and sanctity.

This resonates deeply with me. Having come from an evangelical childhood and then evolving until I found myself among the Unitarians with their unique and beautiful worldview, these words are an inspiration to me. *A Religion of One's Own* rewards me with numerous examples of that kind of challenge, from page one to the end. In fact, books like this prompted me to continue evolving my definition of spirituality until I arrived at my most succinct iteration: Spirituality is the movement toward truth, beauty, and goodness. That definition is broad enough to include multiple worldviews, perspectives, and religions. It works for me. That definition is a result of years of study, reflection, and mindful evolution. My earlier definitions of spirituality were more sectarian and religious. This present definition is more world centric; it leaves room to include others who see things differently. By studying different experiences of spirituality, I have come to my own pathway.

Poetry as well has shown the value in books and studying. Emily Dickinson, for example, has left a legacy of wonderful work. Her poem "There Is No Frigate Like a Book" was written in 1873 before the advent of modern transportation. She wrote in the days of sailing ships that took the wealthy to exotic lands others could only dream about. This poem still speaks eloquently to modern audiences. Emily Dickinson writes:

> There is no Frigate like a Book
> To take us Lands away
> Nor any Coursers like a Page
> Of prancing Poetry—
> This traverse may the poorest take
> Without oppress or Toll—
> How frugal is the Chariot
> That bears the Human Soul.

Emily Dickinson expresses the same thoughts and wisdom I'm trying to convey. We can all undertake pilgrimages, journeys, and exotic vacations without having to climb aboard a frigate or airplane; we can learn vicariously by reading and enjoying breathtaking photography and films. The inspiration acquired by sitting in an armchair in our homes can be just as exhilarating as the inspiration acquired on the heaving decks of a ship or the narrow seats of an airplane.

Individuals who adopt a practice of reading widely and studying multiple perspectives develop an openness required to grow spiritually. This practice offers solutions for those who say they are frustrated and uncertain about how to approach others whose viewpoints differ. We will be rewarded with a deepening of our interior life, which will allow us to face seemingly insurmountable challenges.

In this chaotic world, there is a growing interest in searching for something to help us with our modern-day crises and challenges. The COVID-19 pandemic has produced an uptick in resources to help us cope with our "new normal." People are more ready to respond, now that our "normal" daily activities have been curtailed so abruptly. Hopefully this pandemic will teach us not to be so frightened by the prospect of spending time alone with ourselves. We now have the opportunity to be introspective, to meditate, to relax, and to study.

Throughout my life and my studies, two men named James Adams have had a tremendous impact. One is James Luther Adams and the other is James Albert Adams.

James Luther Adams (1901–1994) was a Harvard professor who became influential in twentieth-century American Unitarianism. He was an intellectual who helped articulate the philosophy that resulted in the modern Unitarian Universalist movement. I first encountered his writings when I lived alone in Ann Arbor, Michigan, and to my good fortune began attending the free-spirited Unitarian congregation. This exposure to the Unitarians expanded my thinking, and I began to see many new perspectives. During those emotional early Sundays when I felt all alone on a new voyage, out to sea, and concerned about where I was going to land, these writings calmed me and inspired me to keep sailing. I observed and studied the Unitarian ways. It was a significant time of growth for me. I will forever be grateful.

The second man, James Albert Adams (1930–2015) was my father. I have met only two or three people in my life who I considered absolutely pure souls—he was one of them. Through his ministry as an evangelical local pastor, he gave his life to caring for individuals and he was beloved by his congregants. He avoided the harsh theological tones of many in his religious movement, and instead he walked with loving intention through each day, responding to each person and every need. He helped his parishioners solve whatever problem weighed on them. Most of his congregants were lower-middle class working people without much formal education. He became their advocate when needed, their counselor when called upon, their solace in grief, and their celebrant in good times. My father had an impressive personal library, and he read widely outside the boundaries of his sectarian beliefs. To me he bequeathed the love for reading, reflecting, and studying. I pushed the boundaries of thought much farther than he did, but he was nonjudgmental in his approach to those who believed differently. I was extremely fortunate to be raised in a household with this beautiful man.

My purpose is to bring to you, my reader, a natural or intrinsic pathway to help you navigate through life with whatever worldview you embrace. The reason The

Path applies across all categories and belief systems is because it focuses on preparation rather than destination, on movement rather than perfection. It holds the promise of a path to calmness that can infuse our lives even in turbulent times.

Our culture is spiraling downward due to many factors, one of which is technology's pervasive influence. Our attention spans are shorter, our thoughtful reading is less, and our distractions greater, mostly due to the addictive nature of our mobile phones and all the accompanying applications. All of these factors work against our understanding about how to live a fulfilling life. All of this raises the questions: How are we to stay calm during chaotic times, and what makes us happy over the long haul?

STEP THREE ACTION PLAN

Continue your path by growing your capacity to study. The resource section at the back of this book offers excellent starting points among a sea of possibilities. Begin slowly and thoughtfully, keeping an open mind. Be aware of new insight as you read and study. Your spiritual pathway will look different from anyone else's—and that is the way it should be. You are unique and special, and so are your experiences and your journey.

I like to read authors who are less sectarian and whose writings explore questions I have yet to resolve. I read slowly with an orange highlighter at the ready, marking anything that resonates with me, anything that is unusual or extremely well said, questions I may have, and points I disagree with. I review my favorite authors regularly and enjoy the same book over and over. If you don't enjoy reading books and this step does not appeal to you, all is not lost. You can benefit from gifted teachings online through a wide array of resources, many of which are included in the resource list at the end of this book. But there is no substitute for actually reading a book.

THE PATH STEP FOUR
REFLECT

*The real voyage of discovery consists not in seeking
new lands but seeing with new eyes.*
Marcel Proust

A friend of mine goes to an annual meditation retreat in upstate New York where he spends a weekend alone with his thoughts (reflection). He looks forward to talking about his life with other participants who attend the same week each year. Over the course of years, they have developed deep and transparent friendships, which encourage authentic and vulnerable reflection. He reports how healing he finds the experience.

The format for meditative retreat settings is instructive for all of us. The days consist of sessions where participants learn together, interspersed with times where they are asked to reflect on what they are experiencing. Exercises may include further reading, walking slowly and thoughtfully, different forms of meditation, artistic activities, and writing. Retreats are now widely available throughout the world, as well as online. They can be well worth the time and expense.

Each of us can find ways to reflect deeply on our own activities throughout our days. When we read the newspaper, we can ask ourselves about the messages and their delivery: How does the news make us feel? How does it motivate us to respond? What encourages us to become more active? When we hit an errant golf or tennis shot or we feel we have stumbled into a controversial and overcharged discussion, we can remember to observe our physical and emotional responses. When we feel we have responded poorly in certain situations, we should ask ourselves: how do I improve, what lesson can I learn, should I change my ways? These kinds of responses help us develop introspective habits that encourage personal growth.

The American middle class simmers with conflict just under the surface of our lives. On the one hand, we pride ourselves in our ability to see, understand, and respond with help for those who suffer. We try to be compassionate citizens through our conversations, our occasional protests, our letters to the editor, our contributions to nonprofits, and other forms of activism. But on the other hand, we enjoy the privileges that the richest culture in history offers. Most of us aren't ready to sacrifice some of these privileges in order to help solve the major problems. We love our air travel, our multiple private vehicles, our meat consumption, our possessions, and our Amazon purchasing power. But some of our capitalistic habits of consumption will have to be reconsidered. Whenever changes occur in a society, a community, or a family, individuals experience growing anxiety. All of those privileges will be questioned and tweaked as our culture moves into the uncertain future.

The COVID-19 pandemic and the current toxic political environment will, I hope, motivate us to be more reflective by improving forms of communication that are more centered on wisdom and science. We need to discuss and create alternative, healthier, and wiser ways to live. How can we enact improvements in our society? We must ask ourselves that question, and then act on the answers.

Reflection helps us accept the need for change. It also helps us realize that the resulting changes may be for the good of others. Contemplative reflection can offer us the reward of lower anxiety. The modern process of reflecting also aligns well with ancient practices. This step in The Path is infused throughout the spiritual journey. Step one of The Path is meditation. Step two is to slow our lives and strive for quiescence. These qualities are necessary in order to achieve the best results in mapping out a calming journey in the midst of an increasingly chaotic world. Reflection accompanies each step. But reflection goes even deeper and more extensively than meditation sessions. It must be a regular and intentional part of life throughout each day. Reflection requires us to incorporate step three as well— what we've seen, read, learned, and experienced—and forge a path that works for our lives in a deeper way than we might have before we started on The Path.

Western culture teaches us that the wisest people are those who have quick answers, or the most degrees behind their name, or are in positions of power. But the great enduring spiritual masters throughout history have resisted those quick answers and the solutions proposed by the powerful. They favored personal reflection; the ability to contemplate their condition in full awareness of the difficulties they faced. Combining the ancient practice of reflective thinking with our

modern scientific sensibilities gives us the best opportunity to solve problems. We shouldn't feel rushed to
find solutions but rather relish the slow, contemplative
movement forward. When this happens, we become
increasingly more comfortable with ambiguity and uncertainty.

Meditation and reflection also increase our ability to see things from multiple vantage points. When
this happens, we will become aware of new and more
creative ways to move forward. This willingness and
skill to see things from new approaches must be developed over time. Our inclination is to default to our
current worldview and resist all other possibilities. We
often look for those perspectives that affirm what we
already believe; we resist looking at the positions that
oppose our thinking. We should intentionally work at
expanding the views and options. As we mature in our
new practices, we begin to cherish the growing ability
to explore a variety of viewpoints. An example from
our school years was found in our high school debate
teams. The best debaters loved taking the side that
they personally opposed, because it helped them grasp
truths from different understandings.

In the realm of politics, we find it difficult to come
up with creative new paths forward when both sides
are so certain of their answers. Certainty is a killer of
creative thinking. Many conservatives in politics and
religion are wary of doubt. Liberals, too, cling to their
certainties, which often makes them disparage those
who think differently. When we embrace healthy doubt,
our new thoughts open up new possibilities. When the
scientific community expresses doubt and skepticism
of the status quo, exciting, life-changing discoveries
are made. Exploration has an element of doubt in it.
When the people of Europe thought the earth was flat

and believed that anyone sailing far enough out to sea would eventually fall over an infinitely large waterfall, it was only because of doubt and skepticism that certain sailors ventured out and "discovered" new lands.

Humans have reflected on how to develop more meaningful ways of living since early in our evolution. The ancient pathways were often very religious in their orientation, but new approaches are helping us move into the next level of understanding. These evolving ways of thinking are very modern and useful for helping us reflect on today's diverse world. You may not relate to some of the ancient ways as much as you appreciate some of the more modern approaches like The Path, but all are instructive for us to review.

Let me briefly describe this evolution by highlighting just three of many approaches that have been articulated down through the centuries. The first is *The Rule of St. Benedict* composed around 512 CE. The second is the *Examen* of Ignatius Loyola, the founder of the Jesuits. The third is an entirely modern path, one especially geared to those who love nature. Day Schildkret presents this approach in his book *Morning Altars*.

Nursia, a community about 40 miles from Rome, was the home of a religious community founded by St. Benedict. *The Rule of St. Benedict* was written as a way to help those who wanted to follow in the footsteps of Jesus. Its fifty or so chapters cover every facet of the ways in which followers should live together in a community. It defines four kinds of monks, what the qualifications for leadership look like, rules for good works, and twelve steps to heaven. The Rule of Benedict lives on today; it became the foundational document and the inspiration for the Benedictine Order within the Catholic Church. Sister Joan Chittister is possibly the most widely read spiritual writer among today's Benedictines. A powerful advocate for women within the Catholic Church, she writes that she yearns for the day when women will be ordained into the priesthood. She carries forward the ancient Rule of Benedict in a modern context at her monastery near Cleveland. Her reflections are an inspiration to millions. Through her prolific writing she continues to inspire and speak to the masses. One of her recent books is titled *The Time Is Now: A Call to Uncommon Courage.* She has written many books and has a great number of readers.

The second approach invokes Ignatius of Loyola, founder of the Jesuit Order, whose members are followers of Jesus. He lived in the sixteenth century and dedicated much of his life reflecting, like Benedict, on what it meant to follow Jesus. After a period of deep reflection, he developed a way for his followers to more closely align themselves with his vision of Jesus. He composed the *Examen,* the spiritual exercises necessary to help his followers in their daily practices reflecting on the life of Jesus.

One of the more famous modern Jesuits is the late Henri Nouwen, the Catholic priest, professor, and pastor who taught at Notre Dame and then became a pastor at the L'Arche community in Canada for disabled individuals. His writings are amazingly wonderful spiritual letters and books written by and from a deep and gentle soul. Our current pope has been a Jesuit since his ordination into the priesthood in 1960.

The third approach focuses on nature. It is modern and secular—and in recent years I have found resonance with this way of looking at spirituality. When I discovered *Morning Altars,* an exquisite volume written by Day Schildkret, I was excited to show my friends Sue and Rich. They love nature and are committed to helping preserve the earth. They enjoy walking the shores of Lake Michigan in what they call their "happy place," in Charlevoix, "up north," as they say in Michigan. When I showed Sue the book, she promptly ordered her own copy and now it is one of her treasures. For Sue and Rich, nature provides a soothing and healing time after they have engaged in meaningful social justice activity.

In words and photos, *Morning Altars* describes Schildkret's seven-step *Practice to Nourish your Spirit through Nature, Art, and Ritual*. He describes how after a devastating loss in his life, he began a ritual of taking long walks in the wilderness with his dog. He began to notice nature's details more deeply. Over time, he developed an artistic ritual, creating mandalas (symbols that often originate in a dream, representing the individual's search for completeness and self-unity). The word "mandala" means "circles," referencing circular drawings that symbolized creativity and the power of existence. They are symbols of the connection with the self and the universe at large.

He photographs them, then releases his ownership of these intricate creations for others to enjoy as they pass by. Schildkret describes how his practice convinced him that he belonged to something greater than himself. Inevitably, the winds and rains and other forces in the natural world cause the mandalas to disappear. Nature is responsible for the altars' creation and for their destruction.

In the introduction to his book, the author points out, "a way through these troubled times can be found in beholding the ordinary and smallest of things." His creations are made of flowers that have fallen to the ground, leaves, mushrooms, twigs, and other natural objects he finds on his meandering walks. The mandalas are stunning in their beauty, as his photographs attest. He calls them "morning altars." He defines them this way: "An altar's purpose is to sanctify something and offer it up to a higher source and without even thinking about it, that's what I was doing with my grief."

Like Schildkret, we, too, can marvel at the things of beauty in our world, and we can reflect with new eyes on our own neighborhoods. The things we see with new and softer eyes will provide inspiration and a path to calm in this turbulent time. Schildkret uses the famous Jewish Rabbi Abraham Joshua Heschel's phrase "radical amazement" when he describes the process he uses to search for nature's masterpieces, which he will use as he creates his stunning art. He describes the joy of being "radically amazed" each morning as he opens his eyes and realizes he has another day of consciousness in a place where he can find and create such beauty. His advice for us applies no matter what scenery we awaken to each morning.

Morning Altars reminds me of the sand mandalas we saw on a visit to Nepal a few years ago. Buddhist monks in the Tibetan tradition have a practice of creating very artistic mandalas, forming circular patterns using colored sand and ground stone, which become beautiful art. The work takes a group of monks several weeks to design, and when they are complete, the sand mandalas are celebrated with formal ceremonies. After viewing and contemplating the beauty, the mandalas are ritualistically dismantled. The materials are collected and transported to a river, where they are released back into nature. The meaning behind it all points to the transitory nature of material life.

Reflection is often rewarded by moments of new clarity. A *New York Times* headline caught my attention because the title of the story started with "Aha moment led to …". The actual article wasn't important to me. What struck me was the use of the phrase "aha moment." As we meditate, we slow our response time, quiet our minds, and reflect. At that point, we are more likely to encounter these "aha moments of the soul."

Historically, we have used the phrase "aha moment" to refer to the moment a scientist discovers, in a moment of clarity, how the dots connect, and a new fact is discovered about our universe. Entrepreneurs and inventors often speak of the moment when they realized a new way of doing something. In a flash, new ways of understanding open up to them, and to the world. "Aha moments" change lives forever, and new inventions and learnings become part of our world's evolutionary march forward. But in recent years I have realized the possibility of these special moments happening throughout our lives. I anticipate these moments, because they convince me that my understanding has deepened. When I suddenly realize something I never had thought of before, I feel exhilarated.

Rarely, if ever, do I hear anyone talk about an "aha moment of the soul." I've heard individuals talk about an evolutionary growth, or deepening in knowledge, but I like the imagery of "aha moment." I live for "aha moments of the soul," when I'm reading or contemplating something and suddenly a new insight emerges. I regard these as treasures. Maybe I have acquired a new understanding or a new way of describing something that comes to me out of the recesses of my brain as it processes all the information and experiences that I shove into it. This is the promise of reflection.

There are two kinds of "aha moments": One is a vivid insight that is recognized suddenly and the other is an intense enjoyment of the unique qualities of the work of artists or writers. Such a moment was captured by NPR's Krista Tippett, host of the popular radio show *On Being*. She was interviewing the Irish poet David Whyte in 2016 when he confessed, "I felt literally abducted by poetry…carried away, never to be the same again." That, my fellow pilgrim, is an "aha moment of the soul." It is eagerly anticipating an experience that captivates us completely and transforms our understanding. David Whyte went on to say that one can never go back. A new perspective has arrived and a deeper truth has emerged. Life is forever altered—and that makes living exciting! Sometimes the "aha moment" is forced upon us by the trauma of life. Such has been the case with some who have suffered failure and in the process rediscovered who they really were meant to be.

These "aha moments of the soul" cannot arise out of a rushed, hurried, anxiety-filled life. They arise out of a reflective, knowledgeable, creative side of life that can only develop by walking an interior journey like I describe here in The Path.

Another anonymous and wise writer observed:

Reflection leads you to quiet and to stillness. But it also leads you to want to teach or to speak that fire that Jeremiah talks about, the fire that the prophet has inside. You don't want to keep quiet, because you feel you've discovered something really important, truthful, wise—some wisdom—and you want to share it.

Now that we have explored Part 1 of this book, Being, which discussed ways to deepen our understanding of our interior lives by meditating, slowing, studying, and reflecting, we are prepared to move on to Doing and the final three steps on The Path. Doing is the movement toward action. This part of the journey starts by dealing with our shadow. Then it moves to the explicitly outward action of Giving. Finally, it ends in an activism that works for each of us in our own unique way.

STEP FOUR ACTION PLAN

Life is full of important milestones. After each critically important moment, we should take time to reflect about the deeper things we are experiencing. Many seekers find journaling an excellent way to reflect and record progress, challenges, insights, and of course, "aha moments of the soul." Journals can be particularly insightful when we recognize our blessings and express gratitude.

PART TWO

DOING –
The Path Toward
Compassion
and Action

THE PATH STEP FIVE
DISCARD

Wake Up, Grow Up, Clean Up, Show Up
Ken Wilber

*The more our darkness is avoided, the more it grows
within us, waiting like a volcano to gush out
at any unexpected moment."*
Lonerwolf website

My wife and I were fortunate to be able to take a trip to Japan and Vietnam in 2019. The flights were amazingly long, and the destinations were stunningly beautiful. My eyes have been opened to the rich diversity of our world by experiencing other cultures. I would hate to live in a world where everything is homogenized into a bland sameness. These two countries gave me added appreciation for their unique and profound cultural identities.

In Japan, the cultural traits of cleanliness, orderliness, and calmness are evident—qualities I highly value. The nation's spotless buses, trains, and subways stand in stark contrast to the loud and dirty subway, air, and highway systems we often encounter in the United States. I would not suggest that Japan is a perfect society, but these traits are particularly refreshing. Everywhere we looked we saw cleanliness, orderliness, and calm in action. The Japanese decluttering expert Marie Kondo has revolutionized the lives of many Americans with her advice on how to get rid of unnecessary treasures and trash. People around the world have adopted her KonMari tidying method as a way that leads to a simpler, more peaceful, more meaningful, and even Zen-like existence. Let's discuss discarding the trash in our own interiors as energetically as Marie Kondo deals with the trash in the interior of our homes. This step is vital for the process of living a fulfilling life and creating calm in a chaotic world.

Ken Wilber summarizes the process of enlightenment and maturity by using four succinct, powerful injunctions for us: "Waking Up, Growing Up, Cleaning Up, and Showing Up." This chapter gives a brief overview of these four aspects of maturity and expands more fully on the cleaning up part, or as I call it, the Discard step of The Path.

"Waking up" is the process of coming to new realizations and evolving into a more mature and comprehensive understanding of life. The Buddhist tradition refers to this stage as enlightenment; other traditions refer to it as wisdom development. Waking up may mean embracing a new and up-to-date understanding of the word "spirituality."

The University of Minnesota founded the Earl E. Bakken Center for Spirituality & Healing dedicated to well-being and spirituality from a secular and modern perspective. I love the non-supernatural and modern definition it promotes:

Spirituality is a broad concept with room for many perspectives. In general, it includes a sense of connection to something bigger than ourselves, and it typically involves a search for meaning in life. As such, it is a universal human experience. Something that touches all of us.

This understanding of spirituality makes room for what has been called "spiritual humanists," people categorized as individuals who don't believe in the supernatural and yet love their fellow man and work to preserve the earth. Spiritual humanists feel connected to something that is bigger than themselves, and they continually work at bringing meaning to their lives. I encountered many who fit this description when I attended the Unitarian Universalist Church of Ann Arbor, Michigan. That time was such a growth period for me; I discovered that there are many ways to live a spiritual life. Whether a person is Christian or secular in orientation, political or apolitical, young or old, "Waking up" is necessary if we are to flourish as human beings.

"Growing up" refers to the process of moving from simple explanations that were good enough for us as children but fail to reflect the multidimensional aspects of adult life. "Growing up" could also be considered a significant theme within this chapter. It requires us to discard old beliefs and images. When we do this, we can go beyond a literal perception of the world.

When our grandchildren Parker and Izzy visit us at our house on the lake, we always enjoy a pontoon boat ride together. When they were between five and seven years of age, the games we played on the lake were filled with fun. We teased them about sea monsters lurking in the water, creatures who wanted to bite off their toes. We stopped the boat in the middle of the lake, and they clambered up on my lap as I dangled my feet in the water. I bounced the children up and down on my feet, holding on to them tightly, but pretending their little toes were going to be bitten off by the terrible monster. They loved the pretend game and filled the air with their shrieks and laughter. They always knew it was pretend, but they wanted the excitement of the game every summer during those formative years. Mythological tales have lessons for us. Social scientists and storytellers throughout the ages have recognized that these tales are essential for our development.

Many take this evolutionary step when they grapple with religion and its attendant mythologies in their lives. They move in new and creative ways to bring their childhood religious teachings in line with what they now know about the world as adults. Some fundamentalists fail to understand the drive to reinterpret the supernaturalism of older religious forms into images that speak to the modern mind. However, increasingly more individuals attempt to reconcile the ancient and the modern when they choose to live within the context of the Christian experience while at the same time honoring science. This process of evolving in our understanding of religious language is a part of the growing up that is needed in order to fully live in and engage with the modern world.

John Shelby Spong is a great example of someone who insisted on reforming the outdated language of the Christian faith, particularly relating to the dogma that was developed in antiquity. In one of his early books, *Christianity Must Change or Die*, he argued that Christianity was in desperate need of a new modern reformation or it was in danger of dying. His last and twenty-sixth book published in 2018 is titled *Unbelievable: Why Neither Ancient Creeds Nor the Reformation Can Produce a Living Faith Today.* Unfortunately, John Spong suffered a serious stroke just before the publication of this work, which sadly brought his writing and speaking career to a close. However, his wisdom and insight remain as vital and compelling as they were the day he described this spiritual journey. He says:

> I long ago walked beyond a literal interpretation of the Bible, but I do not feel the need to abandon the Bible or to suggest that this book no longer has great worth for me....
>
> I long ago moved beyond what I call creedal theology....

But he maintained the hope that he could translate Christian insights into a "coherent form" for modern readers. He adds,

> I long ago moved beyond the worship patterns of the thirteenth century, which portrays God as a parent figure who needs to be flattered or a judge before whom I am compelled to grovel on my knees in penitence.
>
> I believe I have experienced God as the Source of Life.... If God is the Source of Life, then the only way I can appropriately worship God is by living fully.
>
> I believe I have experienced God as the Source of Love.... If God is the Source of Love, then the only way I can worship God is by loving wastefully.

We all have different ideas about what "living fully" means, but it is analogous to beauty—we know it when we see it. Spong's definition of "loving wastefully" is loving with your entire being, sparing nothing, holding nothing back. Loving wastefully is a part of the growing up process. It is less and less about me and more and more about others. As we truly mature and grow up, we get much happiness by "loving wastefully."

Spong borrowed Paul Tillich's phrase "The Ground of Being" to explain how he experiences God. Spong says: "If God is the Ground of Being, the only way I can worship God is by having the courage to be all that I can be." I found this to be such a highly motivating thought. His credo, "Live fully, love wastefully, and have the courage to be all that I can be," should be carved over the doors of every school and university in the country and printed on refrigerators around the world.

Sarah Hurwitz, a *Wall Street Journal* columnist, wrote "Religion for Adults Means Embracing Complexity" (Sept. 29, 2019), in which she points out that in the realm of religion, many of us have "rejected the kiddie stuff, but never bothered to replace it with an adult version." She continues,

> We need to find clergy whose spiritual depth is matched by intellectual depth; who understand that faith at its best is a form of protest against the self-absorption, materialism, triviality and cruelty of modern life; and who are comfortable uttering the phrase "I don't know." In short, when it comes to religion, many of us still need to grow up, and that means doing the seeking, learning, and grappling required to make these traditions our own.

How right she is!

Let's follow up on that brief introductory description of Ken Wilber's stages, "Waking Up, Growing Up, Cleaning Up, and Showing Up." The specific task of this step of The Path is concerned with cleaning up. Cleaning up, or Discard, requires the all-important work on our shadow side. In his book, *Integral Life Practice*, Wilber calls it "cleaning out the basement." And the shadow, Wilber says, "refers to the 'dark side' of the psyche—those aspects of ourselves that we've hidden from ourselves.... We've pushed it out of our awareness." They soon develop into neuroses, which are unhealthy ways to live and form relationships. He adds,

> The ancient spiritual traditions don't adequately address the psychodynamic shadow. In fact, one of the big mistakes the spiritual traditions make is to assume that practices such as meditation can transform the whole individual, whereas in fact they generally leave out some very important aspects of the self, including and especially the shadow.

The shadow, as he sees it, holds everything we prefer to hide. These are often emotional reactions and impulses we learn early, in our formative years, everything from rage to envy, greed, selfishness, lustful desires, and the drive for power. Most of us don't recognize these characteristics as a problem within ourselves, and yet we try to hide them from others and ourselves. We have to exert conscious effort to become self-aware. To do so, we must begin to recognize our shadow side, deal with it, and move toward a more fulfilling life experience. This stage requires important work.

When I was a college student working part time at UPS, one of my friends made me so angry that I shoved him up against a truck and demanded that he stop his aggressive actions toward me. After years of maturing in my reactions, I now respond very differently in uncomfortable confrontations. Now, I try to be more thoughtful in my response. My work at discarding the trash has been a result of years of evolution at work in my interior life. It is also an ongoing process and has the potential to trip me up even now.

The musical group Imagine Dragons has a popular song called Demons in which the following lyrics are repeated several times:

> When you feel my heat
> Look into my eyes
> > It's where my demons hide
> > It's where my demons hide.
> > Don't get too close
> > It's dark inside
> > It's where my demons hide
> > It's where my demons hide.

If we decide to engage in this step, we work at discarding the trash from our lives. Shel Silverstein's famous poem says of trash, "It filled the can/it covered the floor/It cracked the window/and blocked the door." We can choose to remain passive or aspire to become enlightened. We can retain our childish responses, or we can be adults in our understanding of the world. But to live full and fulfilling lives, we must be aware of those shadow sides of our personality that often derail our progress.

Certain characteristic reactions are rooted in the

earliest years of our lives. For instance, grandchildren say and do the funniest things as they are developing. Our three-year-old grandson Trey is no exception. He takes in everything that is said and then repeats the words in humorous ways. The innocence of children as they experiment with language is endearing to all those who love them. We laugh about the way Trey seems to have the verbal acuity of a five-year-old, but the emotions of a three-year-old.

A few weeks after turning three, Trey was quite advanced in his verbal skills. His mother moved him from a crib to his new "big-boy bed," and it didn't take long for him to offer to help his mother change the sheets. She videotaped that first attempt on her phone. To her credit, she always encourages him to try things on his own. He was trying to tuck the fitted sheet on his new bed—and we all know how that goes, even for adults sometimes. Trey didn't have the sheet going the correct way. In frustration, when he realized that it wasn't going to fit, he exclaimed "Dammit!"

We all laughed at his first use of that slang expression, knowing there wasn't anything wrong with it. But this example illustrates the truth that as we get older, we learn to discard language that isn't helpful, whatever that language might be. I am still learning this lesson as an older person. Discarding the parts of life that are holding us back is a good thing and a lifelong challenge. We are often prevented from progressing by failing to allow ourselves to become vulnerable, by refusing to let others talk, or by speaking over them. The list of other foibles is endless.

The Discard part of this journey I am describing is an essential step in our development. As we've seen above, it may involve discarding old notions from childhood and exchanging them for adult knowledge.

But, Discard also requires us to be alert to, and vigilant about, evaluating our shadow side. It is entirely possible to be awakened spiritually and yet held back by psychological baggage we brought into adulthood, either from childhood abuse or other traumas. These situations are often baked into our personalities and reactions. Sometimes they come out in angry responses when unhealthy anger is uncalled for. At other times, negative traits such as anger, jealousy, and competitiveness prevent us from developing uplifting friendships. Demons from early life traumas need to be faced. But we have more resources at our disposal now than ever before to help us in this effort to work with our shadow side.

For instance, counselors focus on cleaning up and addressing our shadow side in order to help us deal with deep-seated anger, unhealthy relationships, and boundary issues. They encourage patients to hold up a mirror in front of their eyes and reflect on their lives in ways that help them finally come to grips with their shadow side.

Another of the most advocated practices to help us deal with our shadow work is through journaling. One very positive feature of our available technology is that we can find help for doing shadow journaling online accessed through our tablets or phones. Just enter "shadow work prompts" and you will find many examples of how to get started. These types of therapies and activities can help us move toward becoming fully actualized individuals. Life then has more energy, is more uplifting, and feels more content.

Not only is discarding important for individuals, it is an important process for entire cultures. When enough individuals do this work and critical mass is reached, the entire civilization is propelled forward. Every category of people, ages, ethnic cultures, and social norms can find shadowy areas needing cleaning up and discarding. Psychologists recognize the critical importance of this work for our development as fully whole human beings. Students of Integral Philosophy and the work of Ken Wilber look at every stage of cultural development, from traditional to modern to postmodern, identifying healthy values at each stage, as well as their respective pathologies. Certainly, our grandparents' "traditional" generation was neither entirely healthy nor full of pathologies—like us, they exhibited a mixture of both. The modern age encompassing the lives of our parents and our own generation, exhibits some healthy aspects of life, but also our pathologies. We can see the same phenomenon in the postmodern youth of today: a combination of healthy and unhealthy habits. In the chart from Integral studies that I've included below, we can see examples of the values and pathologies of each stage. We would do well to recognize what lies within ourselves and our own worldview.

I like to think of myself as understanding and valuing the positives of postmodernism, as well as valuing the positives of the previous stages of traditional and modern values, but full implementation is a work in progress. Sometimes I am successful at highlighting the positive values in others, and often I find myself looking at the unhealthy aspects of those with whom I am dealing, tainting my interactions. Only when I look at the virtues and values of my friends, colleagues, family, and political opponents do I begin to see possibilities that I didn't see before.

Using both sides of the political spectrum as an example, consider a liberal's disdain for all Trump followers by equating his foibles with all the followers instead of looking at the values they espouse such as love of country and a wish to protect their livelihood. On the other hand, a conservative may look at many liberals and see people who seem to tarnish our history by focusing on misdeeds of our forefathers and not seeing that the liberals really just want for us to treat each other better than we often do. The chart on the opposite page illustrates this point. It shows pathologies and virtues of each of the primary worldviews that individuals in our culture adopt. We often find ourselves only looking at the pathologies of an opponent rather than their virtues.

At this point, I want to illustrate pathology by focusing for a moment on a publication of which most Americans are unaware. While perusing my favorite bookstore in Denver, the Tattered Cover Bookstore, with its wooden creaking floorboards, old chairs, and comfortable sofas, I found an interesting magazine, one that employs a very unusual art genre called Brutalist Art.

The entire magazine is filled with photos, drawings, memes, and words that follow a story line from page one to the last page. There are no ads. This magazine is making a statement in its entirety, intended to disturb the reader. One page announces, "We're stuck

World Views: Values and Pathologies

TRADITIONAL VALUES	MODERN VALUES	PROGRESSIVE VALUES
Loyalty to Family/Country	Individual Liberty	Environmentalism
Duty & Honor	Human Rights	Diversity & Inclusion
Sacrifice for Common Good	Rule of Law	Social Justice
	Achievement/Prosperity	
	Economic & Scientific Progress	

TRADITIONAL PATHOLOGIES	MODERN PATHOLOGIES	PROGRESSIVE PATHOLOGIES
Racism	Environmental Degradation	Anti-Modernism
Sexism	Economic Inequality	Reverse Patriotism
Homophobia	Nuclear Proliferation	Divisive Identity Politics
Authoritarianism		Self-Righteous Scolding
		Tyrannical Demands for Reform

Source: Compiled from writings on integral theory
by Jeff Salzman and Steve McIntosh with permission.

in a period of aesthetic and moral stagnation." There is nothing unusual with that observation, but the many disturbing images that accompany this statement are created by artists who are not focused on "style, tone, or ambience, but rather shock, tempo, rhythm." All the images portray death and destruction, alongside vulgar words and images that are meant to shock and challenge the status quo of consumerism, environmental destruction, and war. Again, there is nothing particularly wrong with their stated purpose—in fact, we need more people engaging in these worthwhile efforts—but the execution was jarring. A couple of examples might illustrate this. One image is of the Nike logo with large red letters that overlay it reading "God Hates You." Another image is a black and white photo of a prisoner of war who had been brutalized and left to die. The enemy soldiers were walking by the dying body and laughing. One cartoon portrays a friendly face saying, "Good morning," and the next person responding with "(expletive) you!" All of these images are interspersed with sayings like, "We've lost touch with reality, with nature, with one another...that's why we're in total post-truth meltdown now...."

The thoughtful, well-written articles made it clear that the authors hoped to incite major cultural change. The presentation is an extreme pathological version of what I've seen among some of the postmodern individuals of today. They recognize the problems facing their generation, but feel a sense of hopelessness, believing the capitalist and corporate systems fail to work for everyone and are depleting the finite resources of our planet. They are calling for a revolution to overturn those systems that they consider oppressive, but they often don't offer thoughtful solutions. Great art has always challenged the status quo; I would never suggest changing that—if anything, we need more of that challenge. But what I am observing is that this magazine, as well as other media and activists, are frequently reacting to culture with pathologically extreme language and art, that is ineffective and produces little or no change for the better. If great art is supposed to lift you to something higher than yourself, then it only stands to reason that poor art may drag you down. Perhaps poorly conceived art is the shadow side of the art world. Day Schildkret offers impactful advice: "Let your words be as beautiful as the art you make. Eloquence, too, is food that can nourish deeply."

A shadow side has emerged when Americans engage in political conversation. Art, as mentioned above, often mimics society at large and our political discussions have also sunk to new levels of pathology. All of this has culminated in the accusation being thrown around that opponents are offering "fake news" rather than accurate information. This is happening among friends and family, driving damaging wedges between people. The accusation of "fake news" is often used rather than an engagement in dialogue. We are seeing increasing unwillingness to tolerate an opponent's viewpoints or to find value in even a measure of their perspective. We have turned disagreement into actual hatred of our opponents. The January 6, 2021, attack on our Capitol gave us a foretaste of what's to come if we don't address our shadow side as a culture. This phenomenon will require intense shadow work about our political discourse. Only by doing this shadow work and increasing our tolerance for differences will we see a better path that leads into the unknown future. We really do need to evolve into a better version of ourselves.

Arthur C. Brooks has written a book that addresses these growing schisms in the United States. On the inside cover of *Love Your Enemies: How Decent People Can Save America from the Culture of Contempt,* he writes:

Divisive politicians, Hateful pundits, Angry campus activists, Twitter trolls: Today in America (in juxtaposition to the well-known phrase military industrial complex), we have an "outrage industrial complex" that prospers by setting American against American, creating a "culture of contempt"—the habit of seeing people who disagree with us not as merely incorrect, but as worthless and defective.

Brooks goes on to explain, "Anger plus contempt equals disgust." Our society today faces that challenge. Rather than merely disagree with one another and then work toward solutions, we are divided into camps that look at our opponents across the aisle with contempt—and the contempt all too often turns into disgust. The result is an unwillingness to see anything good on the other side. Schildkret also observes how we get caught up in "the figure-it-out mind, the judgmental mind, the disbelieving mind, or the fearful 'what if' mind." Sometimes it is even the I-know-it-all mind that is so strong in us that we can't see the value in truly listening to the opposition.

Brooks points out the critical change that must take place: We need to learn to disagree in a more effective, open fashion. Less disagreement is not the answer, but better forms of disagreement actually move us to better political and cultural solutions. Perhaps this challenge to disagree more effectively and compassionately is part of the cleaning up or discarding we require, as individuals, and by extension, as a culture. When we are with friends and family, we often are silent, or argumentative because we haven't learned how to engage in productive conversation. Part three of this book will offer some help.

Living a fully alive existence in Discard means balance—balance in all aspects of our lives. My friend Bill probably lives one of the most balanced lives I've ever encountered. He and his wife, Debbie, have structured their lives in a way worth emulating. I see a balance between work, family, exercise, friends, passion for hobbies, and spirituality—a balance I have seen in few others, including myself. When Bill speaks, I hear each of these categories of life talked about with passion. Many stories abound, usually set in a humorous context. Their family always figures central in their lives with multiple trips a year to visit kids and grandkids in New Mexico and California. Bill exercises diligently by climbing onto his road bike in good weather and cycling many miles per week. He organizes a large group every Saturday morning to ride over 30 miles around a local lake at a very fast pace. His passion for photography, particularly of wildlife, is beautiful and composed nicely, and he tops his to-do list off with a set of spiritual practices that puts most of us to shame. It is certainly inspirational for those of us who know him. Examples of this kind of balance offer direction in an age where our culture urges us to "just let it happen" haphazardly—or worse yet, express ourselves in language and actions that inspire few.

When we see someone who has great balance to their lives, we can assume that they have done the hard work of discarding the trash or shadow side. A nicely balanced life helps us discard those voices in our head that demand we stop our progress. Balance is a key to a happy, healthy life, as Bill so aptly demonstrates. If you too, wake up, grow up, clean up, and show up, you will achieve a balance that will serve you well in life.

Discarding your shadow side may seem onerous and daunting, but the results may be revolutionary for you. The process should actually become enjoyable, as you become aware of all aspects of your life and all possibilities for your future, a future of balance and healthy living.

The final part of the process that Ken Wilber outlines is Show Up. Finally, after we have woken up and grown up and then cleaned up, we are ready to show up, to become an active participant in activism for a cause. Or perhaps we are ready to develop a particular passion for something new. If we try to show up without mastering the other steps of our journey, we may diminish our effectiveness. Show up, or activism, will be discussed more fully in step seven.

~~~

STEP FIVE ACTION PLAN

To make an effective first step in the Discard process, you might decide to talk with your spouse, support group, close friend, or professional therapist about your shadow work. A frank conversation over lunch might be enlightening and open new and unexpected doors for self-awareness. The people closest to you might surprise you with their insights and offer appropriate readings or suggest that you find a counselor you can trust to talk with about the issues that need resolving. Either way, Discard is a valuable exercise, with nothing to fear and endless rewards to gain. Now let's move on to step six, which is all about the exhilaration of giving to others.

THE PATH STEP SIX
GIVE

Eat half, walk double
Laugh triple and
Love without measure.
Tibetan Proverb

The greatest pleasure I know, is to
Do a good action by stealth, and to
Have it found out by accident.
Attributed to Charles Lamb

My great friend Phil is considered a modern-day saint by many who know him. His life partner, Maria, is quite saintly herself; she shares her generous spirit with friends and strangers alike by preparing outstanding gourmet meals and always offering a warm and welcoming spirit. After finishing medical training in Chicago, Phil served the Battle Creek, Michigan, community as a family doctor. He led a highly successful career, then retired from his practice and moved to Portland, Maine, where he and Maria could be near their grandchildren, who live on Peaks Island, in Portland's Casco Bay.

Their daughter, Mira, recounts a story passed down to her. One night when Phil was walking home from the hospital after a long day of rounds, he was confronted by a would-be bandit, demanding his wallet. You would have to know Phil to appreciate this, but his calm and collected demeanor was able to render the threat harmless when he responded kindly and said something like, "Hey, buddy, I'm sorry, I don't have my wallet on me. It is obvious that you must need cash more than I do. If you come back to my apartment with me, I will write you a check."

This story is as authentic as its main character; it illustrates the way Phil has lived his entire life, a life of giving to others. Even though he and Maria now live hundreds of miles away from Michigan, they still reach out in caring ways to individuals who are in need in their former community.

The COVID-19 pandemic is demonstrating the giving spirit right before our eyes. When the early epicenter of the virus in America, New York, began to see frontline doctors, nurses, and hospital personnel get sick, they called for volunteers to help. The hospitals were overrun with so many sick patients that even a healthy staff could not handle the load. As soon as the word got out, twenty thousand volunteers descended upon New York, offering to put their lives on the line in order to help fight the pandemic. Newspapers, news shows, and social media reported many other acts of giving to neighbors, friends, and strangers. Some of the more inspirational actions of citizens have been musical performances by professionals as well as amateurs, who share their talents online. Zoom choirs with four-part harmony have helped uplift us and carry us through these days. Solo artists in the confines of their homes join their voices, with the aid of technology. Drive-by visits and celebrations popped up, along with entire neighborhoods banging pots and giving affirmation at 7 p.m., each night, so frontline workers know they are appreciated and loved. Strangers offer to pay for another's meal in take-out lines. People wear masks to protect themselves and others. These "random acts of kindness" demonstrate the feeling that we are all valuable neighbors during this world-wide pandemic. In fact, the most common phrases we all hear these days are, "We are all in this together" or "This demonstrates that we are one with all of life on earth."

Time will tell if permanent change will come out of this, but there is growing hope that we will be more concerned about those who are on the margins, those who don't have the finances, networks, or adequate living conditions to sustain them. The poor and people of color have provided the bulk of the low-wage frontline grocery and delivery services, and that population has been hit hardest. My hope is that this Give section will have a beneficial effect on both givers and receivers as we walk through life. We must increase our willingness to give even more than we have in the past.

Religious texts, of all faiths, ask and answer the question, "Who is our neighbor?" The answer has been affirmed: Anyone we encounter is our neighbor. Anyone who is different is our neighbor. Anyone who has another viewpoint is our neighbor. The needs of our family and our closest friends are apparent, but what about the person on the street corner with the cardboard sign? We find it too easy to pass them by. And yet we have heard the statistic that half the people in our country are living paycheck to paycheck or they have no job at all—and the numbers have grown exponentially since the coronavirus spread to all corners of the world. Too many of our neighbors have few reserves and are unable to sustain an unexpected expense.

To our credit as a society and individually, we outpace many other countries in giving to charitable causes that are often recommended through our houses of worship or local organizations. Usually, our giving involves a few hours a year of volunteering and a few dollars—but let's admit the fact that neither our volunteering or our monetary gifts hurt, nor do they come close to matching how we spoil ourselves by indulging in our wants that are far above our basic needs.

We have also seen some good examples of selfless giving, gifts that far surpass the norm. In my hometown, we have an annual award called "The George Award," an honor bestowed upon an individual or group that goes way beyond most of us in giving to those in need by creating programs or systems that fill a void in the community. It stands for the phrase "Let George do it" as a way of not committing ourselves. That is the kind of giving that our increasingly desperate world needs. That is the example that we can model in our own way, right in our own neighborhood.

Step six in The Path is a necessary part of this journey of wholeness, calmness, and peace in turbulent times. Before we can give, though, we must learn to love others unconditionally, without regard for our own desires. This is what author and retired Episcopal Bishop John Shelby Spong calls "loving wastefully."

Mother Teresa's life was just one example that illustrates even further Spong's point. She was in a religious order that encouraged its members to give up everything for the poor, but if you look closer, you can find something that is applicable to each of us in modern-day America. Mother Teresa didn't change the situation in Calcutta from a macro perspective. She looked around each day and tried to help the person who was in front of her. She didn't ask them what bad decisions they had made. She didn't think, "You made your bed, so now you must lie in it." She simply and lovingly reached out in kindness and respect to help her neighbors through that day—and often that was their last day on earth. So, the question is this: How can we achieve something like Mother Teresa's level of generosity right here and now? How can each of us "love wastefully" right where we are?

One noble trait of Americans is our enthusiasm for helping those in need. We can find many ways to do this. In the next step on this journey, Act, we will discuss options to get involved at the systemic level. But here let's speak about the personal day-to-day actions of our lives, when we are just going about our normal activities. There are innumerable ways to help as we look around. We simply need to think creatively. We rise to the occasion frequently when our society or other countries are hurting. The outpouring of loving actions during the COVID-19 pandemic are demonstrating the love and creativity of the human spirit. Encountering people in need of assistance has become commonplace in our community and in our nation; news sources show us so many struggling to make ends meet, keep roofs over their heads, and find food to feed their families.

In his best-selling book, *The Second Mountain*, David Brooks affirms, "Joy is found on the far side of sacrificial service. It is found in giving yourself away." He explains that our culture has stressed individualism to the extreme, which has left us with a state of tribal allegiance rather than a wider, more inclusive caring, in which we seek ways to serve others. And yet, it is only by giving to others freely and unconditionally that we can begin to heal our nation. He says, "Whenever I treat another person as if he were an object, I've ripped the social fabric. When I treat another person as an infinite soul, I have woven the social fabric."

I have been noting examples of how everyday heroes can express their generosity, because the possibilities are endless. The creativity I'm observing is both astounding and impressive. Each time we reach out to another we are helping to heal our culture. We need to keep our eyes open and stay alert for opportunities to prove we care for the strangers we walk by each day. A great example was shown to us by *Time* magazine when for the first time they chose a "Kid of the Year" for 2020. Gitanjali Rao, a fifteen-year-old student and scientist from Lone Tree, Colorado, was given *Time's* honor as an exemplar of tremendous giving to others in creative ways. Gitanjali said in an interview that she just wants to create programs and apps that will help with many current problems, and her energy has been a success. Rao said in an interview with the Associated Press, that even though science is increasingly being questioned, "It's pursuit is an essential act of kindness. The best way that the younger generation can benefit the world." She has certainly made great contributions to the world with her three most famous creations. Tethys is a device that measures the amount of lead in drinking water. Rao was inspired to create this device after hearing of the Flint water crisis. She was ten years old at the time. Gitanjali went on to create a diagnostic tool called Epione to give an early indication of opioid addiction. And finally, she continues to advance in her giving through science by using artificial intelligence to detect cyberbullying at an early stage.

Another way to give is through conversation with those whose values differ from our own. During the divisive campaign leading up to the election of 2020, I worked at devising a way to speak with those who held very different views. I decided to try my theory on an unsuspecting young man, because I felt he might be on the opposite side. We were at a small family wedding pre-COVID, and it was possible to speak to everyone present during the course of the event. I began to engage him in small talk and discovered that he was a full-time stock person at the local Walmart who lived with the groom's cousin.

I started by gently mentioning that some people in my own political camp drive me crazy with their attitudes. I explained to him how I had gone to a rally for the other side, the one he represented. I started by admitting the pathologies of my own side, and I realized that my theory was working. As we talked in gentle tones, not bashing the side that we didn't agree with, I noticed that he began to lower his defenses, and proceeded to discuss issues authentically.

It was possible for me to offer the gift of conversation to a person from another political persuasion, but first I needed to exhibit vulnerability rather than salesmanship. This became a great lesson. The added benefit was that we left that conversation as new friends, rather than emerging red-faced from an argument about politics or silent because of discomfort.

Let me mention another example of this phenomenon. My son-in-law, Jeff, has a cousin who comes across as very strident in his political views. For several years this stridency made conversation difficult. Recently, Jeff decided to make a renewed effort to communicate using some of the strategies I am laying out in this book.

Rather than being into a "I'm right and you are wrong" approach to conversation, it has become more civil by being more curious about the other's perspective. Over time, the defenses have begun to drop and good conversation is developing. Jeff has been willing to exhibit some vulnerability which makes this possible.

You may ask if this plan works with those who are belligerent and continue in that style of confrontational conversation. It probably won't. Our culture has to grow out of the mess that is created by taking sides and aggressively discounting anything that comes out of another camp. What we need to do, if we are to be successful in engaging, is to identify those who agree that there are better ways to disagree than those ways we've currently been using in our conversations. Our goal is to build bridges of conversation from one individual to the next until a critical mass of people are communicating in better ways. We can indeed grow our culture to the next level of maturity and development. Maturing in our dialogue will make it easier to locate like-minded people who will be willing to discuss important issues. These new and better conversations will be healthy and focused on creative ideas rather than winning an argument.

It will be helpful if political and religious leaders will learn these lessons and use their tremendous platform and example to lead the nation in this evolution. But in order to realize growth in a culture, the change must be evident in a growing number of individuals until it becomes more the norm than the exception. Some make the argument that our political leaders simply portray the attitudes of their constituents. There may be some truth in that which makes it even more incumbent upon us to change the style of rhetoric at the personal level. Our national leaders need to use their platforms to set a higher standard of communication for us to follow. Unfortunately, that doesn't seem to be the case, so once again, we each must do our part to change the trajectory of our country.

We can give by listening to others respectfully, by treating them as individuals with something important to say. Observers of our culture tell us that too often we aren't listening well—or at all—to each other. In a *New York Times* article titled "Lessons in the Lost Art of Listening," author Kate Murphy offers tips on how to listen in a more careful and empathic way:

> "This is all fueling what public health officials describe as an epidemic of loneliness in the United States.… Good listeners ask good questions.… The idea is to explore the other person's point of view, not sway it.… Consider listening a kind of meditation."

We can bestow the gifts of our respect, time, and attention to those who have different opinions. To do this, we must commit our full attention to what others have to say. Let me explain what I mean by using the example of discussing our political thoughts with others. Most Americans carry their political feelings, as the saying goes, "close to their chest." We have been advised to avoid two topics—religion and politics—in polite company. But those discussions happen anyway, often with outcomes that are not productive.

Let's start by describing liberals and conservatives in a general way and use the descriptions that Steve McIntosh uses in his book *Developmental Politics*.

Liberals frequently have a problem with hubris (arrogant pride), derision, and "holier than thou" attitudes. They hope and work for a better world with more diversity and a healthy environment. Many conservatives don't want to even discuss issues with liberals because they feel like they are being talked down to. Liberals have a problem with compromise much the same way that conservatives do. Liberals have no problem talking the accepted party line and reacting sarcastically to the pathologies they see on the conservative side, an attitude that is not helpful. The problem with conservatives is frequently an unyielding certainty, and a fear of the future direction of the world. They just want things to stop and return to an era where they imagine things were more settled. They don't want to be reminded of all the sins of our culture; they value patriotism, God, and family. It is easy to see why so many discussions don't end well when you view both sides from this macro perspective.

Additionally, Richard Rohr has described his disappointment with many liberals and conservatives in one of his weekly email articles (Jan. 12, 2020) from the Center for Action and Contemplation:

> My great disappointment with many untransformed liberals is that they often lack the ability to sacrifice the self or create foundations that last.... Too many conservatives, on the other hand, idolize anything that appears to have lasted, but then stop asking the question, "Is this actually bearing fruit?"

But as I've mentioned before in referencing Arthur Brooks's discussion, we don't need less disagreement, we just need better disagreement. Opening true lines of communication starts with the individual. We decry the lack of civility in Washington, yet we have little tolerance ourselves with those who differ in their views at the local level. My hope is that we will each strive to become creative in adjusting our practices when we are confronted by those who hold different political or religious views.

There are so many ways to give to others. We've been discussing giving by engaging in meaningful listening and conversation at the personal level. So now let's turn to a bigger issue and discuss how to give in relation to the environment. Many people are joining the movements to protect the environment, wildlife, and humanity from extinction. These are all very noble efforts.

Great writers have been referenced throughout this book to help you move from general ideas to specific actions recommended by experts, mystics, and activists.

As Wendell Berry notes in *Our Only World*:

> If we are serious about these big problems, we have got to see that the solutions begin and end with ourselves. Thus, we put an end to our habit of oversimplification. If we want to stop the impoverishment of land and people, we ourselves must be prepared to become poorer. We must understand that fossil fuel energy must be replaced, not just by "clean" energy, but also by less energy.

We have countless ways to give back. Some exercises I would suggest for environmental consciousness require some thought, resolve, and action. Do some research on organizations and programs dedicated to saving the earth—but realize that you have simple methods at home: recycling glass, paper, and cans; cutting out or down on the use of chemicals and aerosol sprays; planting flowers, bushes, and trees that attract birds, butterflies, and bees; monitoring your consumption of water and electricity; picking up trash along roadways; walking or riding bicycles rather than hopping into the car for short-distance runs; using recyclable bags rather than plastic bags. For those who want to take an even bigger step at the personal level, become vegetarian or vegan. The biggest challenge falls on our ability as a culture to make the political decisions that will have the desired effect.

The opposite of giving is taking. We all can take quite effectively—from family members, friends, and strangers and from a generous earth. Our life here in America has been blessed for many, particularly if we consider what life is like in Third World countries. In order to help in the world's evolution, we might need to stage a mini revolution in our own thinking and actions. We need to improve our giving skills. Don't forget what many tell us: The secret of happiness lies in giving!

Giving can be summed up nicely with one of many inspirational YouTube videos I watched during the days of the stay-at-home order in the midst of the initial pandemic wave in April 2020. This particular YouTube video features a flashback to Jimmy Durante singing *Make Someone Happy*. People all around us are hurting and having difficult times getting through each day. When we make someone else happy, it creates happiness in ourselves and spreads farther than we can even imagine. That is what giving is all about.

STEP SIX ACTION PLAN

Make a list of the ways in which you give and another list of the ways you take. Be as specific as you can. We have learned to take, often unconsciously, because of our abundant lives here in America. In order to share that largesse and help the world at the same time, we need to increase our skills in giving. Making a list will build awareness of new possibilities, large and small.

Another idea would be to look for someone to engage with, using the new conversational techniques mentioned above.

THE PATH STEP SEVEN
ACTIVISM AND COMPASSION

*What is the relation of contemplation to
action? Simply this: If we attempt to act
and do things for others and for the world without
deepening our own self-understanding, our freedom,
integrity, and capacity to love, we will not have
anything to give others. We will communicate
nothing but the contagion of our own obsessions,
our delusions about ends and means,
our doctrinaire prejudices and ideas.*

Thomas Merton

As I mentioned previously, I come from a family of clergy and activists. My history includes ministers from the Nazarenes, Methodists, Quakers, Mennonites, and the old Pilgrim Holiness on the conservative side and the United Church of Christ on the liberal side of the belief spectrum. Many years ago, my late Aunt Ruth was at the forefront of lobbying efforts to pass the Equal Rights Amendment through state legislatures around the country. I have a photo of her alongside Alan Alda and Marlo Thomas at one event they were working together. My grandfather was part of a group called Flying Missionaries who flew small airplanes into remote villages in New Guinea, Haiti, and other locations, in order to supply hospitals and other facilities that were caring for the needs of their people. My uncle fought against the influence of the Ku Klux Klan while serving in the state legislature in Indiana. My father was instrumental in the founding of the county department of human services whose aim is to give assistance to those in desperate need. I'm proud of my heritage. It had—and continues to have—a deep impact on my life. My relatives shared a passion for reaching out in compassion and social justice causes. But none of us get it right all the time. Our journeys don't aim for perfection—they aim for good intention translated into action.

This section highlights activism in four realms: compassionate activism, social justice, climate, and the arts. All types and levels of activism are integral parts of our world community. Ideally they complement, rather than compete with, each other.

Activism deepens our normal day-to-day giving that we discussed in the last step. From Give we now move to acts that generate awareness, a compassion that reaches out to help others, and actions that push for real change. The act of giving is at the personal level. Activism is often at the larger, or systemic, level.

Religious conservatives are generally more comfortable with compassionate activism. For centuries, they worked from a heart of compassion, both at home and abroad. They built and staffed hospitals and schools, trained farmers in agricultural techniques, funded micro-businesses, and drilled wells—and those are just for starters. While the bottom line for religious conservatism has been the end goal of evangelism, they usually combine that desire with loving compassion for the individuals with whom they work. Compassionate activism has been a major focus of mission work by conservative as well as liberal religious organizations for centuries, and those worthy actions continue today. Since it is a human activity with flawed individuals, there have been excesses of power and greed, or just plain cultural ignorance that have been vividly documented—but that doesn't diminish the good intention or the overwhelmingly large amount of compassionate actions that have helped millions improve their lives. I wonder where we would be as a civilization if not for the millions of compassionate actions over the millennia of our existence. It is a complicated calculation to attempt to figure out if religion has been a net positive or has had a hampering effect upon the human civilization. Many humanists take great pleasure in pointing out the flaws of religious efforts in the past, just as many religious people have little understanding of the virtues exhibited by the majority of humanists. Analysis of this nature entails a complexity that isn't easily grasped.

Modern liberals have a heart for social justice activism, in addition to compassionate actions. Sometimes they have taken this social justice activism to its extreme and have left their spiritual roots behind. When our spiritual roots are forgotten, we often forget about the importance of love as the foundation for all of our actions. In their drive to attack systemic injustice, liberals sometimes exhibit attitudes and behaviors that make them ineffective. Paul Knitter has said from his experience that if our opponents don't know that we love them, then we probably won't be able to have a conversation with them.

Richard Rohr addresses this problem of acting without the necessary interior work in one of his weekly email articles from The Center for Action and Contemplation.

> I met many activists who were doing excellent social analysis and advocating for crucial justice issues, but they were not working from an energy of love except in their own minds. They were still living out of their false self with the need to win, to look good, to defeat the other side, and to maintain a superior self-image. They might have had the answers, but they were not themselves the answer. In fact, they were usually part of the problem. Most revolutions fail. Too many reformers destruct from within.

> He continues: In order to get beyond the categories of liberal and conservative, we have to teach and learn ways to integrate needed activism with a truly contemplative mind and heart.

Climate activism is becoming a desperate necessity if our world is to stay hospitable to human thriving. Climate scientists indicated a decade ago that the earth could not sustain carbon levels of 350 parts per million in the atmosphere. Our atmosphere now has an alarming 417 parts per million—and the number is climbing. The weather is unpredictable—note the record number of hurricanes, wildfires, floods, and tornados. Wet areas are getting wetter and dry areas are getting drier. Cold climates are warming. Polar ice caps are melting. Are we at a tipping point in terms of catastrophic weather events rocketing toward us at a faster speed? This is just some of the evidence around which we must wrap our minds.

David Wallace-Wells makes a good case for the activism that is generated when fear is the motivating factor. His thoughts on climate activism and the fear of rising global temperatures are a clarion call for us to become involved in saving our civilization. In a *New York Times* article entitled "Time to Panic," he says:

> Conscious consumption is a cop-out, a neo-liberal diversion from collective action, which is what is necessary. People should try to live by their own values, about climate as with everything else, but the effects of individual lifestyle choices are ultimately trivial compared with what politics can achieve.

He cites numerous examples:

> Buying an electric car is a drop in the bucket compared with raising fuel-efficiency standards sharply. Conscientiously flying less is a lot easier if there's more high-speed rail around. And if I eat fewer hamburgers a year, so what? But if cattle farmers were required to feed their cattle seaweed, which might reduce methane emissions by nearly 60 percent, that would make an enormous difference. That is what is meant when politics is called a "moral multiplier."

Activist Cara Buckley wrote about a workshop entitled "Cultivating Active Hope: Living with Joy Amidst the Climate Crisis." Admitting that she considered the theme "wildly optimistic," she decided to attend because she was struggling to learn how anyone can cope with the climate crisis. What she concluded was: "Live like the crisis is urgent. Embrace the pain, but don't stop there. Seek a spiritual path to forge gratitude, compassion, and acceptance."

Zhiwa Woodbury, an ecopsychologist, believes that we are collectively experiencing climate trauma, as both perpetrators and victims. The key to challenging climate trauma, she reveals in the article, "Is There a Cure for My Climate Grief?," is by implementing everyday actions and joining wider movements, all the while endeavoring to develop an individual way to face it without allowing it to control us.

> Operating out of fear, anger, and blame burns us out. That is where the spiritual component comes in—to find a way to move to a place not of tacit acceptance, but of fierce, roaring compassion.... There's nothing more powerful than a broken heart, as long as you have a spiritual container to hold it, one of the speakers said. Suddenly, I found myself paying greedy attention to the rustling trees, the flutter of teeny birds. I felt a visceral thrum of gratitude for what still exists, for what has to be fought for, while it can be beheld.

A plethora of books and articles are being written about climate activism. Many actions in our contemporary world are taking place to call attention to the inherent dangers and to halt the headlong movement toward environmental disaster. All types of actions are needed. The problem is so huge and truly existential in nature, but I'm hopeful that we can instill within ourselves the kind of compassion and spiritual depth that will keep us steady internally as we try to inspire others to join meaningful causes.

A young British freelance journalist caught my attention immediately after reading an article espousing the new movement called Extinction Rebellion. I was struck by the journalist's angry rhetoric. He indicated that we were way past the time to reflect, and announced that immediate, transformative change was critical for human survival. His urgency was evident, and so was his colorful language.

Extinction Rebellion is a group advocating for climate change awareness by conducting dramatic protests that disrupt commerce and government. One such example was when they tried to shut down Heathrow Airport in order to draw attention to their goal. The goal is to force world leaders to take the issue seriously. Extinction Rebellion follows on the heels of the movement of young people launched by Greta Thunberg, the Swedish teenage environmentalist who captured the world's attention about the climate crisis. Greta is inspiring young people all over the world to make their voices heard about the environmental catastrophe unfolding. Some others choose to employ angry and dramatic actions, while many others believe they need a thoughtful, sustained effort to educate and inspire a movement. Perhaps a combination of strong anger by some and thoughtful approaches by others working within the system will be necessary to implement radical, positive change.

Rachel Carson, the early conservationist and author of the book, *Silent Spring*, said in 1962, "Humankind is challenged, as it has never been challenged before, to prove its maturity and its mastery—not of nature, but of itself."

What is activism in regard to climate change and the environment? It takes many forms. I am inspired by the young people who started one such movement to help clean up the oceans. 4Oceans is selling bracelets made from ocean plastics in order to fund their efforts at beach and deep-water cleanup around the world. It is a daunting task, but it is also actions like these that motivate people to change. They face a huge challenge to educate the public and create positive vibes for all of us. It is inspirational and helps all of us to feel good about the little things we do locally.

Many other organizations have equally compelling projects and programs—some to educate and some to do the hands-on work of environmental protection. Among the many organizations are those operating both from a social justice perspective and a compassionate action stance. They include: Ocean Conservancy, Surfrider Foundation, Oceana, Sea Shepherd Conservation Society, Greenpeace, 5 Gyres Institute, Oceanic Preservation Society, Take 3, Ric O'Barry's Dolphin Project, PRETOMA, Natural Resources Defense Council, Woods Hole Oceanographic Institution, Blue Frontier Campaign, Bahamas Plastic Movement, and the Environmental Defense Fund. These are a few of the many organizations dedicated to this cause that can all benefit from our time and money in their worthy efforts to clean up our planet. In addition, local organizations throughout the world need like-minded, well-intentioned individuals to serve the needs of their own communities.

The performing and visual arts fields are also important activist channels. Musicians Bob Dylan,

Woody Guthrie, Joan Baez, New Orleans jazz, and the wide array of current rap artists have written lyrics that are strong calls to action. Combined with their haunting or toe-tapping music, the lyrics demand listeners' attention and involvement. As we walked through the warm spring air toward our lodging after an evening meal while visiting New Orleans pre-COVID, we heard lively music emanating from an establishment up ahead. Sitting at the bar of the Royal Frenchmen Hotel and Bar, my wife and I enjoyed the music of Captain Buckles Band. In addition to the normal themes, the lyrics called for activism. Musical activists have been a powerful force in motivating people to hit the streets in protest, as we witnessed during the Vietnam War. And now we are seeing the surge of activist-inspired songs again; they challenge us to confront our most pressing issues.

One of the most compelling true stories I ever heard is presented in the documentary *Searching for Sugar Man*, the story of a Detroit native and musician, known as Sugar Man. When he was young his music reminded some of a young Dylan. He was extremely shy and played in small clubs with his back to the audience. His songs were social commentary. His song *Inner City Blues* speaks of the problems and challenges of the city during the sixties. Due to unscrupulous agents, he spent his life without success, so he supported himself by working small remodeling jobs on houses, living in his old family home in the heart of the city, and occasionally playing in small clubs on the weekend. Little did he know that in South Africa, he had a huge following of anti-apartheid young people. The urban legend that developed said that he had died by suicide while playing on stage. Two music critics in South Africa decided to research what had happened to Sugar Man. To their surprise, he was alive and living in Detroit. They discovered that he went by the name Rodriguez. After contacting him and traveling to Detroit, they arranged a South Africa concert tour. The documentary shows the arrival of his airplane where a limo was waiting to pick him up. He was surprised to learn that the limo was for him and his fans had filled an entire stadium to hear him sing.

Sugar Man was an artist who put his music out there. He had no idea what impact his music was having, but the art had a life of its own that moved an entire nation. It was a real privilege of mine to hear him perform at the famous Ann Arbor Folk Festival a few years ago. Helped onto the stage by his daughter, the crowd joined in a love fest as the old artist, Sugar Man, performed for us.

My perspective on different types of activism has expanded as I've gotten older. The variety of actions I can participate in within different categories has also grown. Two forms of "softer activism" offer ways to educate others and engage in a movement for change. By softer activism, I mean the participation in causes from a less strident perspective. It isn't like going to a protest, but centers more around artistic renderings that make us think at a deeper and more interior and subtle level than physical actions evoke. The visual arts also provide another powerful means of effecting change. Artists are creating mandalas as street art in many cities. Murals, graffiti, window art, and sidewalk paintings are plentiful. During the time of COVID-19, artists of all ages, professional and amateur, began decorating driveways with chalk illustrations. Others painted and hid small rocks, hoping they would remind the finders to enjoy the small, beautiful things life offers, even in the midst of turbulent times. Small art festivals are replete with visual renderings of artists' inner feelings about social issues. Artistic expression in the form of street art is not often thought of as a form of activism, but upon close examination, this media has the power to convey strong messages to visitors and passersby, some of whom never cross the threshold of art galleries or museums.

During our visit to New Orleans, we took a walking tour to see street art in a neighborhood near the intersection of St. Claude Avenue and Music Street, about a mile east of the spots where the large tourist crowds congregate around famous Bourbon Street. We viewed art in the form of murals and graffiti painted on the side of buildings. Sometimes the art had been commissioned and assigned a location and other times it had been created in a clandestine fashion on abandoned buildings. Each piece had a message for walkers, bicyclists, and drivers to see about race, gender, climate, peace, poverty, and many other themes. This art was the work of well-known activist artists from around the world. Some others have become famous for the messages they portray and the artistic expression they use. They give themselves to this cause, often with very little remuneration. The young awareness activist, Kacy, who led us on the walking tour, was very knowledgeable about the artists and their lives and messages. He had just co-authored a book called *New Orleans: Murals, Street Art & Graffiti, Volume 1*. I must admit, I went into the tour with a bit of skepticism, but I ended the tour with an enhanced awareness. It became a highlight of the trip for me. The camera on my phone captured many colorful, powerful memories of this art, and I continue to enjoy the artistry and consider its messages.

Now that we have discussed the presence of and the need for compassionate, social justice, and climate- and arts-focused activism, we need to proceed thoughtfully. A deepening of our spiritual journey is necessary precisely because of what we've seen happening in American discourse in recent decades. Unhealthy anger at a heightened level is a new reality in our culture. Rage and anger are used as a weapon against people in opposing groups and people with different beliefs. This is happening at the activist level, the political forums, and the personal and familial locations within our society. I am not addressing the healthy manifestations of anger. Psychologists work to help us with anger—but that is not what is being referenced here. Americans have developed a bullying type of rage and anger that drives wedges between groups and individuals and makes progress virtually impossible. The events of January 6, 2021, at our Capitol in Washington, D.C., was a jarring realization that anger is alive and growing in the United States. Thankfully, some in the call-out culture so prevalent in recent years are showing signs of evolving into a people that prioritize a deeper integration and appreciation of varying perspectives. The hope is that this trend will continue. Think of the best images that come to mind when you hear the word intersectionality, the commitment to recognize the unique contribution of every identity group. Bullying rage is a serious problem that distracts from the best ideas found in intersectional dialogue.

A *New York Times* book reviewer wrote, "Female Writers Give Voice to Their Rage," in which she pointed out:

There is, unsurprisingly, no consensus on the correct uses of rage, its prescribed application—even its value. For some, rage must be supplanted by love. For others, rage is valuable and must be harnessed: "We need to embrace our rage and allow it to become a source of energy that empowers the type of work we can do, to build a world we want to see."

But these activists all share the backdrop of our age of rage; of far-right protestors marching with torches in Charlottesville, Virginia, and the massacre at Mother Emanuel Church in Charleston, South Carolina.

The use and misuse of anger and rage will be a continuing dialogue. The Path, however, is written to ordinary people who don't typically resort to rage. It serves as a guide for those of us who are trying to discover how to engage in useful dialogue in this era of super-charged causes. The Path doesn't advocate avoidance of anger; indeed, many actions may need the passion of our healthy rage. Our anger is best utilized if it comes along after the process previously outlined, starting with meditation and a slowing of our reactions. We must study the issues, reflect on the issues, and complete our cleanup work before we can address cleaning up others. We must give to others out of love, not self-interest. Only then, finally, should we move into the fray—whatever that might be for each of us.

As Paul Knitter tells us in his inspiring book *Without Buddha I Could not be a Christian*, we must meet our enemy with love; otherwise, we cannot hold a meaningful dialogue. In his riveting account, he describes the better-than-thou, angry attitude he and his group first exhibited during their years as young

American activists in El Salvador—and the harm that attitude did to themselves. He points out that Thomas Merton once said that some of the most violent people he met were social activists who inflicted great harm on themselves and their cause by the attitudes they displayed. Knitter admits his group fell into that trap. Psychologists have pointed out that unregulated anger does tremendous damage to our own interior being in addition to our relationships.

We are often chastised and called out by those who choose anger as their first response, to get into the battle now and follow their lead. We often feel that the cause is worthy, but we aren't sure of how to respond, and we aren't sure we should just blindly follow the example of some of the more strident activists we encounter. The Path can give us the strength to realize that all kinds of responses are appropriate, from behind-the-scenes support to frontline action. Not everyone should chain themselves to fences or stand in the way of bulldozers trying to build another pipeline. Those types of activists have their place, and through their sacrifices and jail time they have moved our discussion to a new level, but the truth is that we all need each other. We all have different approaches to these immense challenges. No single approach will be appropriate for everyone. Whatever approach we take, we must be prepared for the consequences of our actions. For those who choose actions that involve civil disobedience, they may end up hurt, killed, or jailed for their actions. And they may end up creating a new awareness in our culture that leads to systemic change.

The events in the spring of 2020 after the killing of unarmed George Floyd by Minneapolis police has awakened the rage of many people in this country. The restraint by local police and most protesters around the country was amazing to watch. And the country seems to be building a consensus that attitudes and actions must change, even though change is slow to be enacted. We cannot accept any longer the all-too-common use of deadly force against unarmed black people. The call for continuing reform on many fronts is being increasingly recognized.

COVID-19 has also given us the time and opportunity to reflect deeply about what kind of a culture we want to live in. In the past months, we've seen violence in the streets from left extremists and from protesters following police shootings. We've seen violence from the right extreme in Washington, D.C. The protests around the country have spurred us to thought-provoking discussion. The vast majority of protesters have stayed within the bounds of lawful protest, although some have chosen to vent their rage (or opportunism) in destructive ways, by looting and setting fires or attacking our peaceful transfer of power. Each will have to accept the consequences of their choices in these turbulent and explosive situations. We all want good to arise from all of this turmoil, including reform in the way we police in this country. Our hope is that we respond to inequities in healthcare, voting rights, housing, job opportunities, training, education, and healthy food options. The biggest challenge is to reform systemic economic and political inequities. The most likely scenario is that many politicians will hope this all blows over so they can get back to the status quo. Time will tell if the American people allow that to happen.

The key is to have a nationwide, deep conversation, where all these perspectives can be discussed openly. That may be a utopian ideal, but it is desperately needed—and it isn't unprecedented. Nelson Mandela's legacy is his work on behalf of South Africa's efforts to dismantle apartheid. A key feature of Mandela's life after prison was the creation of what they called the Truth and Reconciliation Commission. The commission was not to ignore the facts of all the horrifying actions and violence that accompanied apartheid, and they were also charged with working toward reconciliation among previously opposing groups.

We have our own work to do in the United States. In America we must face up to our past abuses in addition to our celebration of the American experiment in democracy. It is a work in progress, and we can and must do both truth-telling and celebration. In a documentary called *The Social Dilemma*, about technology's pervasive effect on our culture, one of the individuals observed that "we are living in a utopia and a dystopia all at once." We have much work to do.

The point of all this previous discussion is that we need to prepare our interior attitudes and perspectives for agency and for change. That preparation in no way diminishes the existential task confronting us. We can completely understand why anger is the leading emotion with some activists. The problems they are attempting to address are huge and daunting, and they are frustrated when few appear to be listening, let alone joining in the good fight. We can all find it easy to become angry and disillusioned very quickly when those around us seemingly go on with their lives as if nothing is amiss. But what many modern social justice activists are missing is the deep spiritual preparation that The Path offers. These steps will help us all reflect and grow in ways that will make our activist efforts more successful. Knitter points out, "Contemplation—regular practices of spirituality—is necessary both to have a product to deliver and to have the energy to deliver it." Changing the messenger goes hand in hand with changing the system.

Polarization and political identity are two elements dividing and stagnating the American culture. We are so divided around age, gender, finances, race, politics, education, opportunities, and religion that we find it hard to imagine progress on these many fronts. Separate camps don't converse with one another very well. An abundance of new resources in the form of books, articles, and podcasts raises concern over the state of affairs within our American culture. It is evident that increasingly more individuals believe we are on the wrong track as a culture, yet no one seems to know what to do about this fragmented cultural phenomenon. The answer I am suggesting is to intentionally walk The Path, or a similar interior path, as a way to start our efforts to help change our world for the better. We desperately need to expand our ability to understand and tolerate other perspectives. In Part Three of this book, you will also gain some valuable tools in this task. Many of the chapters and subjects overlap and deepen the discussion of that which has come before in previous steps.

The Path offers a journey forward, toward peace, compassion, and action. The Path outlined in these pages applies to everyone: conservative and liberal, religious and nonreligious, young and old. It isn't targeted at the powerful, the elite, and the ultra-wealthy. Nor is it targeted at those leading revolutionary causes on the right or the left of our culture. This path is for individuals who want to do the right thing for themselves, their family, and all their neighbors.

In the preface to their book, *Occupy Spirituality: A Radical Vision for a New Generation*, Adam Bucko and Matthew Fox echo my hope:

We dedicate this book in solidarity with the young everywhere who are seeking a world of values, not power games; of solidarity, not hierarchy; of fun, not dourness; of sharing, not hoarding; of sustainability, not extinction; of gratitude, not regret; of expansiveness, not tribalism; of respect, not domination. May we—elders, mentors, and youth—know we are in the struggle together.

The partnership of these two authors and activists is a great example of how to transcend generations. Adam is a young adult and Matthew is an older gentleman, scholar, and activist. We need to encourage conversation and partnerships that bridge the many interest groups in our country, such as their difference in age. It is possible if we expand our thinking about better conversation. Preparation is critical before action is initiated. The Path is all about preparation and developing our interior lives.

Richard Rohr, the Franciscan monk from Albuquerque, New Mexico, offers daily meditations as part of his work at the Center for Action and Contemplation. In his online article on Tuesday, June 9, 2020, he deals with what he calls "Contemplating Anger" and highlights the words of Mahatma Gandhi: "I have learned to use my anger for good.... Without it, we would not be motivated to rise to a challenge. It is an energy that compels us to define what is just and unjust."

Barbara Holmes echoes his points when she articulates her views on anger:

> We all need a way to channel and reconcile our anger with our faith.... A theology of anger (for communities under siege) assumes that anger as a response to injustice is spiritually

healthy. My intent is to highlight three ways anger can contribute to spiritual restoration.

First, a theology of anger invites us to wake up from the hypnotic influences of unrelenting oppression so that individuals and communities can shake off the shackles of denial, resignation, and nihilism.... Second a theology of anger can help us to construct healthy boundaries. And finally, the healthy expression of righteous anger can translate communal despair into compassionate action and justice seeking.

Healthy expression is the focus of section three, "Becoming," the final leg of The Path. It refers to developing authentic and constructive voices for a chaotic world. Our voices will be calming, civil, and accommodating of different viewpoints. Therefore, they will be able to reach across boundaries that separate us and begin to heal the divides in our country and around the world ...one voice at a time! So, let's now turn our attention to some new thoughts on how to converse in meaningful ways.

STEP SEVEN ACTION PLAN

Make a bookmark of the seven steps in The Path and begin to refer to them on a daily basis. Try to increase your attention to the necessary first step of meditation and then move on to a deepening understanding. Put it into practice at your own pace.

PART THREE

BECOMING –
The Path Toward
Better Conversation

FAILURE WITH MOM

It is not easy to live up to The Path I have set out in this book. My hope is that my writing demonstrates the necessity to try. When I practice the steps, I become closer to the kind of person I want to be. I can feel my interior growth take small incremental steps forward. I become calmer and reflective. My actions are more thoughtful and my love for others is a joyful kind of love that feels great.

But recently I had the experience of failure, of slipping back after taking a few steps forward. It didn't feel good. It reminded me of my humanity on so many fronts.

It started when I went to visit my mom at her independent living facility about seventy miles from my home. That trek is a weekly habit that I look forward to. She is ninety-one years young and very cognitively sharp. Mom looks forward to my visits and we often are able to run small errands together or I take her to her various appointments. On other days we just sit on a bench in the sun or on her little patio and make small talk. My mother grew up in a very religiously conservative home and a very sheltered environment in the heartland of the United States. She retains much of her fundamentalism in religious matters and I normally just listen and smile. My approach to her has been to be positive, not to rock the boat with upsetting conversations, preferring to listen respectfully when she talks about her religious or political beliefs.

On one summer day we were sitting on the bench, when out of the blue she made what I perceived to be an insensitive statement that had its origins in her childhood experiences in the mid-sized city where she grew up. Something in me was caught off guard and I began to unload on her with my shaming reaction to her statement. Then I expanded it to my views of her political feelings. I came across too harsh and judgmental and it visibly upset her. She was not shy in telling me that I was too strong in my reaction. I went away from that meeting feeling like I had not lived up to my own Path. There wasn't any reflection or contemplation. I was caught off guard and my reaction was not loving enough for that situation. At ninety-one years of age, she cannot be expected to have the same perspective I have. I'm the younger generation in her mind and she will never significantly change her positions in what remains of her life. After apologizing several times, we slowly got back to our jovial selves and life has gone on.

I recount this episode to make the point that as much as I believe strongly that The Path offers us a higher quality of engagement with others irrespective of their beliefs, it takes continuing daily effort to walk this path. We will all fail at times; we are human after all. But the effort to improve the way we walk The Path is worth it. I feel much better about myself and the way I engage in this time of crisis after crisis in our culture.

The Path gives me options that are not present in the winner-take-all approach we see around us.

This section of the book is about conversation. The first two sections were specifically about the seven steps of The Path leading us toward calmness as we walk through each day. The Path helps us to be thoughtful in our shadow work, in our generous giving, and in our active compassion or social justice efforts. But in each day of our life, we are confronted with conversation. Those dialogues can end up making us feel energized or depleted—it all depends on how we go about it. Conversation is where our lofty ideals are put into practice. It is hard to engage in loving action without some loving conversation. This section is my attempt to add to the abundance of information about what makes an authentic and healthy conversation.

You will see that there is hope for the human race; hope begins with better conversation. There is hope that we can find a way to communicate with one another that gets us beyond the gridlock and polarization in which we are enmeshed. As I've mentioned throughout this book, we are caught up in an inability to have good conversations at home, at work, at church or other places of worship, in school, or across the table. We retreat into our own private thoughts when it comes to politics or religion because we know that such conversations run the danger of starting a shouting match or doing damage to friendships. Remember Arthur Brooks's statement that it isn't less disagreement that we need, it is learning how to have better disagreement that is critical.

If the first part of calmness and meaning in life is found by following the seven steps I've articulated in The Path, then the way to achieve The Path's ideals in culture starts with improving our personal conversations. In many ways I am suggesting a bottom-up movement in our culture. Our leaders are not modeling the kind of character traits we hope to instill in our children. Something is wrong with a culture when our leaders exhibit less than the best practices of conversation as if it is the norm. The only way to improve our culture's conversational quality is to begin at the individual, then family, and on to the local level. As a culture, we are struggling with how to agree upon basic facts. If we can at least talk to each other in civil tones with an open heart to learn from others, we may begin to reclaim a common understanding of facts and sources.

Another reason we struggle with conversation is because our American culture is changing at an accelerated pace in regard to religion and spirituality. The well-known Pew Charitable Trusts has a tradition of surveying the beliefs of our culture and studying the changes over recent decades. They published their recent findings in the fall of 2018, which included the question, "When you say you believe in God, what do you mean?" In that study they found that while nine in ten Americans say they believe in a higher power, only a slim majority believe in the God of the Bible. In a survey conducted in December of 2017, the Pew American Trends Panel began asking respondents, "Do you believe in God, or not?" Although 80 percent of respondents answered "yes," subsequent questions revealed that just 56 percent believe in the divine being described in the Bible. Roughly a quarter (23 percent) of all the "yes" respondents said they believed instead in a "higher power or spiritual force." And although 19 percent of respondents said they did not believe in "God," half of them said they believe in that higher force. Just 10 percent of those surveyed said they believed in no transcendent force, power, or being. All of these factors demonstrate reasons why organized religion in America is suffering large declines in weekly attendance at church services. On the one hand, we can see changing beliefs of Americans, and on the other hand, we recognize a growing interest in spirituality versus organized religion. The result is likely a major cultural shift that will undoubtedly take decades if not a century or more to fully arrive.

The traditional religions that have been part of the American modern history are declining at a fast rate. New forms of meaning, purpose, community, and ritual are taking their place. The three main worldviews—traditionalism, modernism, and postmodernism—are all part of the tension we feel in conversation with one another. The problem that many social scientists are concerned about is our inability to engage in good and meaningful conversation across the barriers of both the political and religious perspective. We seem to be moving to a culture of separate islands of meaning that are not friendly or cooperative with other islands. These are troubling signs and chaotic times as 2020 has made abundantly clear.

Why does all this matter in regard to The Path? It matters because The Path leads us to interior growth that will help us navigate these uncertain and turbulent times. This section of the book offers us tools to help in conversation with others who may be enmeshed in different silos of understanding than our own.

Authentic and healthy conversation is a requirement for our culture to advance. There are some who will not be able to converse with us due to their allegiance to the "smash the opposition" style of engaging in conversation. When we encounter these kinds of individuals, we are unable to engage in the same way we would with those who are calmer. For the verbally abusive types we may need to walk away. There are some activists who will choose to fight that battle with aggressive opponents. But often we observe the warriors becoming angry and disillusioned about the state of the world after failing in their conversational attempts. The methods I'm suggesting lead to calmness and peace in the midst of chaos. And once in a while, they lead to breakthroughs. New terrain can be traversed in conversation and we can then actually move the ball forward.

~

LEARN HUMILITY

The ancient philosopher Socrates, the gadfly of old Athens who lived about five hundred years before the advent of Christianity, had a message for us that is still relevant. Socrates was the predecessor and teacher of Plato, a prolific writer. We only know about Socrates through the writings of his famous students whose philosophical teachings became very influential in the development of Western and Christian culture. Socrates spent his time teaching the wealthy young men of Athens who were the sons of powerful leaders of that city. His teachings amidst the political upheavals of Athens eventually cost him his life when his enemies forced him to drink hemlock poison. How did he get on the wrong side of his city's leaders? He challenged the hubris of the leaders in his community. His message was simple, profound, and disturbing to many. Socrates used his powerful ability at what has become known as dialectic conversation to teach young men. His primary goal was to get these young, spoiled, and arrogant students to realize that the beginning of wisdom is when you finally arrive at the place where you realize how little you know for certain. His primary lesson was that it is at that point where wisdom begins to grow. I've stood in the Acropolis where some of that history occurred. It is an amazing and awe-inspiring place to visit high on a mountain overlooking the city of Athens. In our contemporary world, we are caught up in a culture of hubris where we don't like to admit how little we actually know. But an amazing thing happens when we listen to Socrates. We then begin to open our hearts to new information and life begins to show us new possibilities.

Pierre Hadot, in his magnificent book, *Philosophy as A Way of Life*, says about spirituality and Socrates:

> The practice of spiritual exercises is likely to be rooted in traditions going back to immemorial times. It is, however, the figure of Socrates that causes them to emerge into Western consciousness, for this figure was, and has remained, the living call to awaken our moral consciousness.

In the end, when Socrates was being quizzed by his interlocutor, Socrates didn't try to teach anything. Hadot wrote: "He repeats, moreover, to all who are willing to listen, that the only thing he knows is that he does not know anything."

He went to his death at ease with himself, and the historical record says he had a smile on his face while his followers and friends were in deep distress over his fate.

In America today, the ancient lesson is a good lesson for us to learn. We don't have all the answers and life may leave us without good choices. But our wisdom and evolution will occur in that moment when we learn to admit how little we actually know. Then and only then can we develop the wisdom of our interior life. Then we become open to new and creative conversations and thoughts.

That is where we need to start when contemplating conversation with those who are different from us. If we can develop a little humility as our starting point, it will set the stage for better conversation. In our capitalistic business-oriented culture in America, we often exhibit overconfidence in how much we know. This shuts down the possibility of good and creative conversation. When that happens, our colleagues begin to withhold their own verbal contributions in the face of our overconfidence. It is becoming very difficult for us as individuals within the American culture to listen to an opposing viewpoint.

Recent examples can be found on college campuses. Before COVID-19 shut down all large gatherings, there were certain comedians who were increasingly deciding not to perform on university campuses across America because the politically correct environment was not conducive to stand-up humor. When nothing is funny anymore, it points to a society in which we cannot speak freely without fear of being shouted down or cancelled due to a misspoken word or phrase. Humor is a needed antidote to our cultural anxieties, and I fear for us if it disappears.

We need to encourage a basic goodwill toward others in social settings that should just be cordial. If good conversation starts by increasing our humility about how little we know, the next step in great conversation is recognizing the evolution in which we all take part.

Takeaway
Conversation with an opponent happens best when
we are humble about how little we know.

HISTORY LESSONS

I can illustrate what an expanding perspective
looks like by giving you a short survey of my evolution
over the years. As a youngster I was immersed in the
worldview of quite conservative and traditional evangelicalism. Our home was an ordinary middle America household with parents who provided us with love
and care. For that I'm full of gratitude. My parents
were very loving and dedicated partners and provided
a stable home for us to grow. We never doubted our
mother's or our father's love for us, and that knowledge
helped my brothers and me to build a good foundation
for life.

From my father's extensive library, I was introduced to my first readings beyond the narrow religious
views of the setting in which we were raised. I fell in
love with the writings of Harry Emerson Fosdick, the
famous founding minister of the Riverside Church in
New York City in the early decades of the twentieth
century. Fosdick expanded my thinking and led me to
other authors such as the Quaker professor and writer Rufus Jones. It wasn't long before I discovered John
Shelby Spong. From Spong, who is calling for a brand-
new modern reformation within Christianity, my
studies took me to the peace churches of Anabaptism.
My great friend and mentor, the late David Helmuth,
taught me much about the simple, peaceful, and quiet

lives of the Mennonites, Quakers, and Amish. These teachings all fit well with my lifelong interest in religion and spirituality with an emphasis on finding our way to our own truth in these matters.

Observing and reading from a diverse selection of books helped me move toward my next internal evolution which came through the perspective of the Unitarian Universalist. Each of these groups introduced me to writers who were thoughtful, articulate, and world-centric rather than sectarian. From Unitarianism I was introduced to Buddhism and then to secular Buddhism as articulated by Stephen Batchelor. I've read and studied, with curiosity, the literature of feminism, queer theology, and modern social justice movements. I consumed these writings in order to build a better awareness as an older, straight, white man. Finally, I found the writings and online resources of Integral Philosophy as written by Ken Wilber, Steve McIntosh, and Jeff Salzman which gave me a framework to understand all of these evolutionary steps in my journey.

One target audience for my writing is the group of people who have left behind the confines of organized religious life. My writing aligns most closely with those individuals who claim the spiritual-but-not-religious mantra. As Spong says, some of them feel as if they are in religious exile. I am walking beyond conservatism, beyond liberalism, and into a new reality that offers a way to talk across boundaries that separate us.

Many authors, friends, and conversations later, I have a renewed appreciation for all of the steps in my journey that led me to where I am today. I don't disparage the evangelicalism of my youth nor any of the stages in between. Each stage had values that have been incorporated into who I am. I've rejected the pathologies of conservatism and liberalism in favor of the beautiful values of each. I've never been more at ease with what I have evolved into than I am right now. My journey isn't about perfection, it is about the process. It is a great place to be. It opens up the meaning of truth, goodness, and beauty each day along with a certain freedom that is very liberating. It is no longer about what I believe. It is about how I am evolving.

Takeaway
Authentic and healthy conversation along our journey of life helps us evolve into better versions of ourselves.

PARTIAL TRUTH

I recently had the privilege of exploring the Finger Lakes region of west-central New York. What a beautiful treasure this area is. During those autumn days, I was inspired by the large rolling hills and colorful forested slopes. Deep gorges that had been cut into the earth by the streams and rivers over the millions of years provided awesome vistas to enjoy.

On one particular hike, I listened to an interactive webinar on my phone while I walked along a forested trail. It probably wasn't the best way to enjoy nature, but it was the only time this important podcast was to be shared. At the end of the segment concerning better conversation during this time of extreme polarities in our culture, the moderators opened up the "chat room" for comments or questions from the audience. I was at the parking lot by this time and I quickly added two things that I thought would add to the conversation about how to engage in meaningful dialogue with those who are different. To my pleasure and surprise, they read my comments on the air and affirmed my input about the concept of "partial truth" or partly correct. Each different outlook in others that we encounter usually has a partial truth wrapped up within it. We may reject the tenets of the person with whom we are engaging, but if we think more broadly, we may discover the partial truth that is contained in their perspective.

This is an important idea to keep in mind and it has an effect upon our attitudes when we are speaking to someone who views the world differently than we do. If we look for the partial truth in what they are saying and think deeply about it, then we will tend to be more understanding and maybe even more accommodating. Humility and recognition of the values of another's perspective go a long way toward great interactions with those who will walk this path with us.

One reason why truth is always partial is the evolutionary nature of all of life. If life is always changing, then the truth today will be enhanced and developed into a fuller expression, which may include things that are true and things that are now considered to be false. Even when there are setbacks, which inevitably happen, the evolution of each of us and life on earth continues unabated.

An emerging field of study, particularly in the United States and Europe, is Integral Philosophy. The concept of partial truth is a foundational observation that Integral has posited. I'm going to share a brief overview from the Integral website, Daily Evolver. The website and podcast were developed by Jeff Salzman, a longtime Integral advocate and popularizer. He hosts a weekly podcast that can be accessed there. If this is your first experience with Integral thought, you may find a perspective you have never encountered before and an interest in learning more about this emerging approach to our current state of culture. Like any new discipline, it takes some study to comprehend, but it is well worth the effort. The basic idea is that all of life in the universe is an evolutionary process, and that includes the interiors of our life.

Integral Theory on the Daily Evolver website says:

> Integral theory is a school of philosophy that seeks to integrate all of human wisdom into a new, emergent worldview that is able to accommodate the gifts of all previous worldviews, including those which have been historically at odds: science and religion, Eastern and Western schools of thought, and premodern, modern, and postmodern worldviews.

> Integral theory builds on the foundations of evolutionary theory. Evolution is well established by science and is noncontroversial for anyone with a modern or postmodern worldview. We know from ever-more sophisticated observation and analyses that the cosmos burst into being about 13.8 billion years ago, first as energy then as matter, arising as atoms and molecules that formed the heavenly bodies, including our home, Earth.

> Integral theory posits that evolution is not limited to the exterior forms of reality (matter and organisms) but is also evident in the interior spaces of reality, namely in the development of culture and consciousness.

> An integral view of history maintains that the collective consciousness of the human race

has evolved through premodern, modern, and postmodern structures, and is emerging into a new structure of consciousness, the integral stage, which is characterized by the ability to think and act from multiple worldviews.

Integral Philosophy emerges from the writings of the philosopher Alfred North Whitehead, the philosopher and poet Jean Gebser, and others. As they observed the human race and our history, they saw that evolution has been part of every aspect of life on earth and even all development within the known universe. With the work of Ken Wilber from the 1960s through today, the Integral proponents have been attempting to synthesize all the major philosophies, religious systems, science theories, and human development, and thereby describe some understanding as to how they all fit together from an evolutionary perspective. To gain a deeper grasp of this emerging field of study, I would recommend the works of Ken Wilber and Steve McIntosh. *The Presence of the Infinite: The Spiritual Experience of Beauty, Truth, and Goodness,* written by McIntosh, is a great book to read after acquainting yourself with the Daily Evolver website. If you are interested in how this new approach aligns with political discussion, read McIntosh's new book *Developmental Politics: How America Can Grow Into a Better Version of Itself.* Ken Wilber's books are also very rewarding, but you will need a deep interest in the details of Integral Philosophy before you will see the value of wading through his intense academic work. Personally, I have benefited from working through these writings looking for nuggets of truth that have brought me great moments of inspiration that I earlier referred to as "aha moments of the soul."

So how does Integral relate to the concept of looking for partial truth in others when we are in conversation? We see it as we recognize each individual we meet as being on a different point in their own continuum of development. Recognizing and honoring the starting point or story that each person brings to the conversation is a requirement for those of us on this path.

Prior to the 2020 election I discovered an article on the website, Patheos, "5 Ways to Find Common Ground This Election Season" by Mark Feldmeir. His third suggestion was, "Don't compare the best in yourself with the worst in others." That syncs well with the Integral concept of partial truth. Instead of looking for the worst part of what our opponents are saying, look for the best version of their perspective. Some call it their values.

A good example of this "partial truth" dilemma is contained in my wife's obsession with calorie count in the food we consume. She is blessed with DNA that gives her a tall and slender figure. She is also disciplined about working out, and that included running three miles every day in earlier years. While I've always enjoyed the aesthetics of her figure, it sometimes drives me nuts when she has to look at the calorie count of every package of food that we purchase. Her body weight never changes more than about five pounds either way, while mine can change 20 pounds easily. As an older man, I have to work to control my waistline. While I enjoy physical activity like bicycle riding and pickleball, I also enjoy my dining experiences. I was raised to love almost any kind of food, particularly sweets. She is much more disciplined in her eating habits, while I can easily consume more than one sugar-laden dessert or candy in a short period of time. For me each bite is pleasurable, and I want to consume more than I should. If I can take a step back and reflect on her habit of calorie counting, I realize that it is an obsessive concern to preserve our healthy bodies as long as possible as we age. Her obsession with calories contains a partial truth that I need to recognize. Understanding partial truth will hopefully help us become more generous in our communicating with each other.

We have mentioned the value of adopting the Socratic message of humility and we have discussed the idea that our friends have a partial truth in what they are saying. The evolutionary nature of all of life is also a thought that helps us with understanding that not everyone is at the same level of development as we are—in fact, others may be more mature in their journey. It is all very humbling and should lead to better conversation.

Takeaway
Conversations with those who are different are most satisfying when we learn their partial truth and value their contributions.

⌒

THE WORLDVIEW OF INTEGRAL

Let's look at the three lenses through which most Americans see the world: traditionalism, modernism, and postmodernism. There are other more ancient worldviews that are represented by words like archaic, tribal, and warrior. But our concern in this book is the three most common worldviews we see today in our culture. Over the past several hundred years, we have seen three distinct stages of human consciousness develop. And now we are beginning to see the emergence of the next worldview or paradigm that offers real hope for becoming better versions of ourselves. It is called Integral by academics. It will undoubtedly be described with different words once its emergence becomes more evident and cultural scientists study it even more closely. Peering into the future is very difficult, and there are always surprises as the reality of lived history becomes evident. But some of the Integral features are beginning to show up in small but incremental steps. The list below shows the virtues of the three worldviews we've been discussing and also the virtues of the emerging Integral worldview. The following list is from the Daily Evolver website.

Traditional is characterized by: Rules, roles, discipline, fundamentalist faith in God or truth, morality, guilt, social conservatism, delayed gratification, and other features. This way of viewing the world is about five thousand years old.

Modernism is characterized by: Rationality, science, democracy, individualism, capitalism, materialism, achievement, secularism, risk-taking, and self-reliance. This way of viewing the world is less than five hundred years old.

Postmodernism is characterized by: Pluralism, subjective view of truth, sensitivity, egalitarianism, world-centrism, civil rights, environmentalism, feminism, and political progressives. This view has been developing for the past one hundred years with a big push forward during the 1960s.

Integral is characterized by: Combining head with heart, being able to hold multiple perspectives at the same time, natural hierarchy, autonomy, systems/complexity, flex/flow, and decrease in fear. This viewpoint has been emerging in an increasingly large number of citizens across the world for the past thirty years. Further study of these stages will reward you with a new understanding of our shared world.

When you look at the levels of development listed above, you see only the virtues of each evolutionary stage. The previous chart in the book highlighted the virtues and compared them with the pathologies of each of the first three stages. The importance of understanding the way culture changes over time becomes clear as we encounter others who see things very differently from us.

If we dialogue with a person having a different political persuasion or worldview, we can have a conversation with them when we both exhibit the virtues of our position rather than unhealthy pathologies. On our side of the conversation, it becomes very difficult to achieve good outcomes when we fail to see their virtues. The same applies to the reverse situation. If they only see us as representing the pathologies, they will misread almost everything we try to say. But if we can broaden our understanding to appreciating what they have to say, then conversations will be much more satisfying. Again, we are reminded not to compare the best in ourselves with the worst in others. What we don't realize is that when they look at us, they only see our weak or negative positions and it drives them crazy. We may not see that we have any shortcomings in our perspective, thus silence or argumentative discussion and unsatisfying outcomes ensue. We've all heard the stories of the family gatherings that have lapsed into ugliness due to overheated and misunderstood ways of communicating across the table. I am not suggesting that adopting this strategy for conversation will convince those who are just plain obnoxious or uninformed. Often it is best to not engage at all in that environment. Be content to stay silent.

≈

Let's now discuss in greater depth the three categories of cultural philosophy or worldviews that I have referenced in this book. Most Americans find themselves navigating through life using one or more of the three most common worldviews discussed here. Some even have elements of multiple worldviews in their approach.

The traditional worldview represents about thirty percent of the American population according to Integral researchers. In this approach the primary motivating values are America's national interests, Judeo-Christian and family values, ethnic assimilation with upward mobility, military stance against threats to our way of life and personal industriousness, and "lying in the bed of your own making." This way of looking at life is a paradigm that has lasted for centuries. In the traditional worldview, a high value is placed on rules and defined roles along with discipline and a more fundamentalist faith in God or truth. Along with those characteristics we see an emphasis on morality, guilt, delayed gratification, and a resonance with social conservatives. The traditional worldview in the 1950s was represented well by the magazine *National Review*. As the famous editor, William F. Buckley, wrote in 1955, "We stands athwart history, yelling Stop."

It is easy when viewed through this lens to understand many of the political conservatives in our country who want things to stop changing so fast. From a religious view of our culture, these are the folks who value the church structure and the standard Christian beliefs that have been established for centuries. When you look at the virtues seen in traditionalists, it is possible to see why our grandparents and previous generations saw the world through this lens. The modern world was changing too fast for them and they loved to harken back to "the good ol' days." If the virtues of that era were a devotion to God, country, and family, a pathology or negative effect might have been a stifling pressure to all act alike.

Modernism is the worldview in which approximately fifty percent of the American population aligns. These folks find themselves somewhere among the modernist philosophy that values entrepreneurship, limited government, free markets, individual freedom and achievement, scientific progress, rights of minorities, and government safety nets for those who need it. They also value capitalism, materialism, secularism, risk-taking, and self-reliance.

The modernist perspective arises out of the enlightenment and has produced the huge advance in science and technology we see all around us today. Even though the modernist movement arose a few centuries ago, it took many years to gather steam until it really took off after the civil war in the United States. Invention after invention totally transformed our way of life. My grandmother told me about the time when she was a little girl in Ohio riding on a buckboard drawn by a horse. She and her sister heard a loud noise approaching that was totally unfamiliar, and around the bend came one of the early automobiles—it was the first one they had ever seen. They laughed and laughed at the strange-looking contraption. Little did they know how drastically that invention along with airplane travel would transform the world in which we live. Now, of course, we take it all for granted. We love and are addicted to the technology of mobile phones. The world is at our fingertips. Social media transcends all the worldviews we are discussing. The pathologies of modernism may include technology's addictive nature and its alienating influence that has become a real problem for modern society. And yet its promise to help us in education, medicine, and many other fields is unparalleled.

The 1960s saw the emergence of yet another iteration in what some call postmodern philosophy, subscribed to by about 20 percent of Americans. The word postmodern is a controversial word and some just lump it in with modernism. But many cultural philosophers see the postmodern movement as a distinct and different movement than modernism even though there are overlapping concerns (as there are in all movements). The traditionalists of our grandparents' generation mostly trusted civic and religious authorities. The modernists built the consumer society we inherited after World War II. The postmodernists question everything including the very essence of truth. Many of them have become skeptical of organizations after the disillusionment from the twentieth century's world wars, the holocaust, the Korean and Vietnam wars, the Watergate scandal, materialism, racism, and environmental destruction. Because of the massive disappointments of all those wars and the disillusionment with political leaders, the postmodernists often act as if there is no objective truth, though few would actually say that. They want to say that each person's truth is just as valid as the next person's truth. This emphasis may have helped us as a culture to break out of the stifling effects of traditionalism and modernism, but eventually this much unfettered freedom and relativity leads us nowhere. That is where we are now. Each person and group has its own truth. Anger and loss of confidence in institutions is growing. The end result of our postmodern experiment is that we are unmoored from our traditional stories. These stories used to provide structure and an essential common understanding to our lives. Some academics call these stories meta-narratives. Most social scientists say that we have lost the meta-narratives that give us meaning. The reality now is that we are free to do and believe what we like. We are free, often angry, unhinged, and anxious.

Philosophy professor Daniel Bonevac quotes the famous author Umberto Eco when he says, "Postmodernism is the sense that the past is restricting, smothering, and blackmailing us." Eco's quote is a popular way of summarizing the philosophical movement that has had such a huge impact upon our world since the 1960s, and it correctly describes the disillusionment of the young with the structures that have been handed down to them. Postmodern individuals don't trust the old structures of politics, religion, and economics. Even art has lost its previous standards of evaluating its quality. Now, as a young artist relayed to me, it is all in the eye of the beholder; anything goes. It is very subjective. The old attempts at objective standards have fallen away for good or bad.

Another primary concern with many postmodernists is a deep concern for the environment. These are often the individuals who champion social justice and world-centric morality. They promote diversity, multiculturalism, and strong affirmative action. They are allies of feminism and LGBTQ equality. They admire natural lifestyles and openly expose America's past abuses such as systemic racism, abusive patriarchy, and globalism's effect on our economy and capitalism on our environment.

This postmodern view of life is growing and is having a huge impact on our culture. The millennials and Gen Xers, who make up approximately 20 percent of the population, are very much captivated by this worldview, but they aren't the only ones. Many baby boomers are also in this camp, especially the ones who value some of the better aspects of the 1960s, such as the questioning of needless war, the freedom to be who we want to be, and the recognition of sexual diversity and identity. It is no wonder that arguments develop in conversation very quickly when individuals have different worldviews. Understanding these levels of development is critical if we want to improve our interactions with others.

Here in the early years of the twenty-first century, most of us find ourselves looking through the lens of either the traditional, the modern, or the postmodern worldview. Sometimes we straddle portions of two of the perspectives. It is apparent that a person with one perspective can completely talk past a person with another, because they see life from an entirely different worldview. This creates the phenomenon referred to as a "culture war," where differing groups angrily and verbally do combat with one another from the safety of their own particular silo of understanding. Instead of appreciating and learning from multiple worldviews we encounter, we are fighting over the differences. We are, in the case of politics, actually disparaging one another rather than creating an atmosphere of mutual respect. And all of that makes the current situation untenable for the future. It makes us uncomfortable when we learn that there are more ways than our own to look at life. Our conversations become less satisfying because of this gap in our understanding. Understanding these levels of development is critical if we want to improve interactions with others. The developmental stage of each of us determines how we present ourselves and how we respond to others.

What I am suggesting and hoping, is that as a culture we will grow our worldview to the next level so that individuals from all perspectives will be able to conduct better conversations. Steve McIntosh advances the argument that the only way we can get to a more healing time in our culture war is by growing our own selves to a new understanding, a new worldview beyond the three discussed here. He speaks of our need to become better versions of ourselves. There are levels to be achieved beyond what we are calling postmodernism. Some cultural scientists have begun to call the next level "Integral."

Takeaway
Multiple worldviews are all around us.
Learning to discern the difference will help us
conduct more satisfying conversations.

~

PARTIAL IS BETTER THAN NOTHING

"Include and Transcend" is a key concept within this new Integral approach. It is a critical concept for the emerging level of culture that provides hope for the future. If we start by realizing that our conversational partner has some truth in what they are saying in terms of their values and history, we then feel more at ease with their verbal habits. I'm not suggesting we appreciate all of their prescriptions for problems, but if we can focus on the values they bring, then we are off to a good start in having a meaningful conversation. If we follow up with that thought, we can include those values in our own understanding and then go beyond them or transcend them into new territory, then we are actually getting somewhere. We will then begin to make progress toward brand new solutions that no one has contemplated before. The best values of two very different people become the seed for the growth of new ideas and new solutions. Our leaders need to learn these lessons and we need to model them at the local level.

The growing Integral crowd sees the values in other perspectives and focuses on those values rather than the pathologies that separate us. And as has been mentioned, it is helpful to embrace the Integral focus on the "partial truth" of our opponents and the idea that we can "Include and Transcend" multiple viewpoints. Include and transcend means that I can deeply appreciate the way I was raised and yet transcend my parents' worldview to new and more personal approaches to life that have meaning for me.

Integral philosophers claim that none of the three worldviews are able to lead us politically or spiritually into the future. Many major institutions in our world are weakening due to the effect of the struggle to achieve a common understanding on how to view our culture. Previously strong religious practices like church attendance are declining, suspicion of government and law is increasing, and huge corporations are contributing to the gap between the rich and the poor. Postmodernism and traditionalism are fighting over the allegiance of the modernist, that large swath of the population who comprise the middle ground in politics. What may happen is that politically we will see-saw back and forth from one election cycle to the next without a consistent vision or coherent path forward. Because of the increasing youth population and the inevitable death of many aging modernists and traditionalists, the demographic trajectory overall may favor the postmodernist in the short term. Can the postmodernists deliver solutions for the longer-term future? Can they even govern? What about a much-needed spiritual vision for the country? Integral philosophers doubt that the three common cultural worldviews have that capacity. As we hopefully evolve toward the Integral vision, the next evolutionary step for our culture, we will see a more positive and useful outlook emerge.

To close this section with a hopeful note, we are beginning to see new nonreligious but spiritual presentations becoming widely accepted. Two examples illustrate what I have dubbed secular sermons. Listening to the poetry of America's first youth Poet Laureate, Amanda Gorman, is like listening to a contemporary and postmodern nonreligious sermon, but full of hope, optimism, and helpfulness. Amanda burst into our consciousness with her phenomenal performance at the inauguration on January 20, 2021. The second illustration of this phenomenon of secular spirituality that is ascending in our society is found in books similar to the works of poet Maggie Smith who just published *Keep Moving*, described online as a book that "speaks to you like an encouraging friend reminding you that you can feel and survive deep loss, sink into life's deep beauty, and constantly make yourself new." Those are the kind of words that bring healing to anyone who reflects on them regardless of one's religious or nonreligious approach to life. We can include our own perspective and yet transcend into new and creative approaches to life by consuming these kinds of messages.

Takeaway
Conversations can help us evolve as a culture as we "Include and Transcend" the three worldviews we encounter.

~~

TRUTH, GOODNESS, AND BEAUTY

The true, the good, and the beautiful are words that describe the ultimate values and virtues mankind at its best can achieve. These words were identified in the age of Ancient Greek philosophers like Socrates, Plato, and Aristotle. The true, the good, and the beautiful are considered to be our intrinsic values—those values that all others derive from. In its formative years, Christianity borrowed heavily from these concepts.

What is true? This has been one of the most important questions in the history of mankind. Within religious circles the language of dogma is foundational to their ideas of what truth is and traditionally includes supernatural beliefs. In the scientific community, truth is based on evidence that all can observe, test, repeat, and demonstrate to others. Science rejects the supernatural in favor of evidence-based observations. In the twenty-first century, new forms of spirituality are evolving that value evidence-based views of the world rather than religious, supernatural dogma. Some contemporary approaches to spirituality value science, and they also value the virtues that have been presented by religion over the centuries without the baggage of strict dogma. These concepts do not mean that they don't find any meaning in supernatural understandings or mythological stories that have come down to them through their family or religion. But if we are aware of the difference between science and faith, we should be comfortable articulating which of our thoughts are based on science and which are based on faith. What is dogma and what is scientific fact? Another distinction to make is: What is history and what is mythology? What is supernatural that makes us feel good and deal with the future, and what is evidence-based information that can be demonstrated to anyone with an open mind? Millions have found great meaning in their faith tradition with its supernatural components. What is important is to acknowledge that those supernatural components are in no way scientific knowledge and shouldn't be presented that way. Just this acknowledgement alone should make conversation more effective across boundaries. We can then converse about facts and simply agree to have our own opinions about matters of faith.

Our concept of the good also evolves throughout life. The language of the good has been translated in religious language to mean the compassion and social justice efforts that are undertaken as a result of religious teachings. The good among the more secular understandings would be around altruistic actions we undertake as humans, such as kindness and generosity. An interesting thought experiment is to consider two viewpoints and how close they really are to one another in their practical application. The first is represented by a book titled, *The Weakness of God*, by modern philosopher John Caputo. This book presents the idea, that many modern theologians posit, that the only way God can act on earth is through human hands and efforts. So that is one side I want you to hold in your mind for a moment. The other is the secular side of altruistic philosophers who don't believe in a religious view of God. These individuals are known as humanists. Within humanist writings is the injunction for all of us to work for the good of society through the use of our hands and effort and also through the use of our resources. When you look at both of these positions side by side you will find that they are literally saying the same thing. It is our effort that changes things in the world through loving and compassionate actions. Thinking in this way is an integral exercise in the sense that a compassionate religious person can work with and have a discussion with a secular humanist who also cares for others and for the beautiful earth that we call home. Instead of denigrating the approach of the other, they can converse and work as cooperative friends who think differently about esoteric things. That is okay!

The intrinsic value of the beautiful also evolves throughout life. The beautiful in culture is where we find our artistic creations. It is the aesthetic part of life. It could be said that it is the part of life that inspires us to higher thoughts. It is emotion, artistry, and the sensual. It is nature and love and music. In my estimation it would be hard to find a song more sensual than Leonard Cohen's rendition of *Dance Me to the End of Love* found on YouTube with 27 million views. With its classical European violin and two beautiful women to accompany him, the song takes you to memories of every experience of sensual love you've ever had. As we've mentioned previously in this book, Thomas Moore in his work, *A Religion of One's Own,* contains beautiful passages that speak to the side of life that is enhanced by healthy sensuality. French professor, Pierre Hadot, looks at the virtuous side of the ancient philosophy of Epicureanism when he says,

> We are to relive memories of past pleasures and enjoy the pleasures of the present.… Epicureanism preaches the deliberate, continually renewed choice of relaxation and serenity, combined with a profound gratitude toward nature and life, which constantly offer us joy and pleasure, if only we know how to find them.

Many of us believe that the beautiful in our lives, whether it be found in artistic expression or sensual experience, prepares us to engage the truth and the goodness that is needed to heal our world.

Steve McIntosh and others have written extensively about these intrinsic values. They feel that the true, the good, and the beautiful are the primary values of any religion or philosophy. What religious systems and all human organizations do, over time, is attach further opinion and dogma to each of these intrinsic values and as time goes along these attachments have become belief systems. The additional dogmas of religion or business or political identity become rigid and codified until we begin to identify the dogma as the truth rather than the original virtues of the true, the good, and the beautiful. It is important to realize that once we get one step removed from these values, it becomes opinion and viewpoint rather than the objective goal of truth, goodness, and beauty. An example of truth would be scientific discovery today with conclusions about the meaning that may be entirely upended by a discovery in ten years that reveals new understandings. The wisest scientist knows that science is always a continuing process of searching for truth. And regarding beauty, what specifically is viewed as aesthetically pleasing in art is constantly changing as standards of beauty change. But the concept or idea of beauty is intrinsic, it is foundational, it does not change.

The helpful thing is that as you understand this, then you begin to see that it is at the general higher level of the true, the good, and the beautiful where we can have discussion across boundaries that have previously separated us. If we are willing to ask what is the truth that others see and how is the good and the beautiful expressed differently from group to group, then we can move to an appreciation of difference.

A real authentic and healthy conversation is one where we respect the personhood of the other. We don't disparage them just because they think differently. We realize that when we attach belief systems to these primary virtues, they become merely opinions that are often unprovable rather than intrinsic truth. It is healthy to have our own opinions no matter how strange the belief system is, as long as it doesn't hurt anyone else.

An example might be that one believes that we can contact the dead through a variety of methods. Science does not support that belief. And yet there are many who live their lives believing they can contact the dead. In the evolving Integral world, it mostly doesn't matter what each person thinks in their own private circles of like-minded people. What matters is that we all respect our differences, and we all agree on some basic paths forward that are good for everyone. There are innumerable weird (from our vantage point) and supernatural beliefs among those who we encounter daily. None of that really matters as long as we admit that those beliefs are not scientifically provable. We then can focus a conversation on the part of life that is provable and helpful for everyone. This is the hope that Integral Philosophy offers for our future that may take us beyond our current conversational stagnation. Once again, the inclusion of the idea of partial truth helps us with these challenges.

Let's apply this to our current political situation. The charges of "fake news" have become a rallying cry for some on the conservative side. On the liberal side, the normal response is an eye roll, which serves to denigrate the opposition as being ignorant. In an integral world, both sides would have a civil discussion about how we are going to demonstrate what truth is. The prerequisite to this kind of a discussion is two people who are willing to discuss that issue in a civil manner. In the absence of civility, nothing good can happen. But if our leaders actually model how to do this, we will be able to advance as a culture in our politics.

So, for instance, let's presume in the discussion it is revealed that the conservatives believe the liberals are pushing too fast and too hard on their agenda around immigration. The conservatives may say they are concerned that we have lost thousands of jobs by not protecting our borders and allowing for low-cost labor to enter our country without good processes to regulate the flow. The liberals may counter that we need to accept the immigrants who arrive at our borders with compassion and welcome because many of them are fleeing traumatic situations in the country of their origin and they add value to our national economy. If both of these concerns are placed on the table for consideration, then the civil and integral discussion will be to honor both positions in coming up with solutions that are more comprehensive and address both concerns.

The discussion can be rooted in Integral Philosophy—the evolving next worldview after postmodernism, a truly evolutionary advancement for civilization. It is a way of approaching life that is positive, hopeful, and does not appear to have a strong shadow side. Integralists believe, and I concur, that if enough people attempt to understand and use integral thinking, our culture will survive in a healthier fashion than we are currently experiencing. Integral thinking isn't about changing one's religion, ethnic, or spiritual tradition. It is about adding greater depth to what you already possess from your heritage. If you have moved away from your heritage, it will add new dimension to your life in ways that will move you toward authentic and healthy engagement with those around you. Integral thinking isn't a new religion or even spiritual path. It is simply a more evolved way of approaching the difficult divisions that are holding us back in our contemporary culture. Integral thinking, as an addition to your accepted faith tradition, is a real enhancement.

Post-progressive is a newer and more accurate title for Integral Philosophy according to Steve McIntosh. When you wish to read at a deeper level, I would direct you to the Daily Evolver website. After you read the introduction and listen to some of the presentations by Jeff Salzman, you may get excited about exploring the cultural observations this philosophy is highlighting. Then you will be directed to the Integral Life website, where you will see a thorough discussion of the theory behind Integral Philosophy. Another newer resource is the website for the think tank Institute for Cultural Evolution. This think tank was created by Steve McIntosh and some like-minded partners including John Mackey, the CEO and founder of Whole Foods Market.

In his book *Developmental Politics*, Steve McIntosh offers a way to advance our culture through evolving to the next level of consciousness particularly in helping us achieve a new way of approaching each other across the many battle lines that have been drawn in our political life. In his previous book, *The Presence of the Infinite*, he discusses the intrinsic values of the good, the true, and the beautiful. I highly recommend both of these resources if the Integral Philosophy resonates with you.

Takeaway
Conversation takes on a higher quality
when we discuss diverse interpretations of
"the true, the good, and the beautiful."

LOVE AND LET GO

I am ending this section of the book with the step that is useful for us all no matter where we are in life. Be loving in our intention and then let it go. Let your efforts go into the universe in ripples of good intention and the universe will be better for it. I worked for two companies whose founders were from India. The culture in India is very different from the American culture. And even though my Indian colleagues were green card holders or actual citizens of the United States, their life experiences and culture were very different from mine. It was a fascinating and rewarding experience for me to interact with these good people.

One of my friends and colleague was a guy named Ravi. I had lunch with Ravi once when I was struggling with how to combine not only peacefulness and calmness, but also action. Ravi explained the Indian spirituality of business to me with these injunctions. Just do the work and then let it go. Don't be anxious about it, just do the best you can in the moment and then let it be. Not every Indian colleague did this as well as Ravi, but it was a great lesson.

First: Love is the goal of almost every spiritual tradition that has ever graced this planet. Wastefully giving of ourselves is the key to making the world a better place to live no matter what religion or ethnicity you claim. There has never been a good substitute for love as the default position as we embrace and engage with the culture around us. This means, in part, focusing on the good of others rather than their negatives, which will eventually create a culture that is worth leaving to our children.

If we want to love others, it is helpful to love ourselves by seeking the kind of happiness that brings self-love along with it. Some call it authentic happiness. Dr. Martin Seligman is a researcher and professor of Positive Psychology at the University of Pennsylvania. His seminal research on well-being has highlighted what has worked since antiquity but is entirely relevant to a modern and secular audience. His YouTube TED Talk called "The New Era of Positive Psychology" is only twenty-three minutes in length but gives a nice overview of the research into what makes us authentically happy. There are several key features of his research into long-lasting happiness. They include times of pleasure that has the shortest life span of these characteristics: social engagement which is a feature of extremely happy people, the ability to get into a flow experience using your strengths, and building a meaningful life using what you do best. All together, they spell true long-lasting happiness. Following these steps throughout life has provided the authentic happiness leading to self-love that many have achieved.

Loving others is the other side of a well-rounded love of life. It starts by really looking into the soul of those we meet. We train ourselves to look for the uniqueness and gifts that they may bring to the world. We might begin to see this in the homeless person on the street corner asking for a dollar to buy some food. When I look into their eyes, I see a real person with the same hopes and dreams I have.

Secondly: Let go. A great benefit of The Path, starting with meditation, is that if done in a mature and thoughtful way, you will begin to develop what Stephen Batchelor calls "nonreactive stillness." This is letting go. Buddhism calls it detachment; Christianity calls it trust in God. This quiet place of rest during times of chaos allows you to have peace even in the midst of an anxious culture. It allows you to begin to appreciate the good things, the virtues of where you've come from, and still relish the place you find yourself in now. It calms anxious moments. Our economic system has an element of judging others based on their financial stability and success. Those who haven't figured out how to make the system work for themselves are often looked down upon by many who have been given plenty. If we can detach just a little from our love of things or property or family, we will be able to open our eyes wider to the needs that we can meet all around us. The great spiritual traditions of the world point toward a certain detachment from the things of this world. If we can become less in love with our next new toy and more in love with the interior journeys of the heart, and more in love with humanity around us, we will be less anxious and more calm. Our hearts will break open in love and acceptance of all those we meet, and the world will move toward healing.

CONCLUDING THOUGHTS

Leave something of sweetness
And substance
In the mouth of the world

From the poem *Cold Solace*
by Anna Belle Kaufman as printed in
Maria Popova's *Brain Pickings* (Feb. 8, 2020)

This book is about spirituality. Spirituality can be accessed by anyone, whether or not they consider themselves religious. A meme (an image, video, piece of text, etc., that is copied and spread rapidly by Internet users) that shows an underwater ocean scene demonstrates the difference between religion and spirituality. Two fish float near each other in a body of water. One fish is contained and restricted in a fishbowl within the large section of water and that one is titled "Religion." The other fish swims in a vast ocean of water and that one is titled "Spirituality." The message? The spiritual dimensions of life are far wider and deeper than any specific religion. Those of us committed to specific religious leanings can find valuable resources to manage our lives, and the same can be true for those interested in a more secular journey. But too often our conversations around religion divide us, rather than unite us. And those who value organized religion often don't see the rich and wide diversity of spiritual expression that is present all around them.

Joan Tollifson offers a good definition of spirituality in her book *Death: The End of Self Improvement*:

> When I use the word spiritual, I don't ever mean spirit as opposed to matter, or spiritual as opposed to secular. Spirituality as I mean it is a perspective that sees all of life as sacred, and by sacred, I mean worthy of devotion, full of wonder, inconceivable, and ungraspable. The kind of spirituality that has attracted me is about direct experience, not belief or dogma, and it is focused on Here-Now, not some imaginary future.

The Path is primarily about spirituality and recognizing attendant beauty and goodness in others; therefore, it can be an enhancement to any religious belief. It is a great add-on to any religious practice; it doesn't diminish personal belief systems. It should deepen and expand beliefs in ways that make life more meaningful, without destroying cherished religious thoughts.

Religious history offers stories and examples of beauty and goodness. One of many is the story of St. Francis, the monk who left a life of wealth and privilege to become mankind and nature's friend. He loved all the creatures who roamed the earth, the flowers of the field, and all people, rich and poor. His story demonstrates a remarkable journey taken in very difficult times, yet his journey led him to immense peace and harmony, and he deeply influenced millions of people who followed in his footsteps. Other examples of individuals from the nonreligious side of things are exemplary of spirituality without religion. Even the famous atheist, Sam Harris, recently wrote about spirituality in his book, *Waking Up: A Guide to Spirituality Without Religion*. Anyone from any persuasion who awakens their interior journey and evolves into a loving example becomes a leader we can emulate.

The book is also about promise. Promise for the future depends upon our evolution as a culture and as individuals. We must evolve into better versions of ourselves, individually and as an entire culture. The Path prepares people to converse with those who have very different views. This means that if we are serious about the interior path that leads to meaningful dialogue, we will actively look to befriend those who are different. If we can figure out how to do that, it will lead to better peace and harmony as well as better solutions for our problems. The famous former basketball great, Kareem Abdul-Jabbar, designed and sells a T-shirt that says it all: "Make a Friend That Doesn't Look Like You…. You Might Change the World."

CALMNESS IN CHAOS

We have a growing need for calmness in the midst of chaos. It is increasingly doubtful that the current state of politics or religion will help us much in achieving the kind of tranquility that will see us through the difficult years that lie ahead. The basic theme of this book is that we each need to begin intentional practices that lead us toward peace and calmness in the challenges of life. The Path is a way to reach this goal.

Meditation is the starting point for our journey inward toward calmness. We then must deepen the practice of meditation by relaxing into our new approach toward life. Following the slowing of our interior pace, we move toward intentional study and reflection. These first four steps on The Path will have a calming effect upon us. We are then ready to do the next hard, but rewarding, work of discarding the interior trash that often holds us back. Then we are ready to give wastefully and act in compassion and/or activism to change our world for the better.

This journey is really about bolstering the strength of our interior lives through meditation and reflection and outward actions like loving wastefully and thoughtful activism. We desperately need to pay attention to our interiors, but we also need to go beyond this work and pay attention to our social dimensions. Our friendships matter immensely, our family connections matter deeply, and as writer Choire Sicha put it: "People really want to hang out, work out, make out, and dance it out." (*New York Times*, Arena Section, article titled "What's Happening to Us?")

This book does not present the message that things will be easy. Whether your life turns out to be easy or hard, rich or poor, or a mixture of both, the need for an interior calmness during chaotic times is a need for everyone. If you add The Path to your individual approach to life and grow your ability to converse in authentic and meaningful ways, you will be able to handle whatever life brings you. The Path is about process not perfection, preparation rather than destination.

Those who wish to walk this journey should pack their metaphorical bags, lace their walking shoes tightly, and prepare for astounding vistas and imaginative new perspectives.

Joan Tollifson notes this idea, as expressed in a cartoon that spoke to her near her sixty-fifth birthday. "It pictured a long line of cute penguin-like creatures waddling in single file across a vast plain that extended as far back as the eye could see, and at the front of the line, the creatures have arrived at the edge of a cliff, a very steep precipice, and the caption reads, "Man, I guess it really was about the journey and not the destination." She goes on to apply the lesson, "When the future disappears, we are brought home to the immediacy that we may have avoided all our lives—the vibrant aliveness Here-Now, the only place where we ever actually are."

It is against the backdrop of the place where we are now—our current reality of pandemic, protest, and political upheaval—that I want to conclude this book with a note of hope brought to us from fourteenth century England. Julian of Norwich, quite possibly the first woman to publish a book, lived as a young woman during tough times. The city in which Julian lived was a small city of about twenty-five thousand residents in 1330 CE. That time frame in England was characterized by huge upheaval in politics and religion. There was constant warfare and epidemics were rampant. The plague known as "The Black Death" ravaged Norwich and killed approximately 75 percent of the population. In the midst of all that suffering and death, Julian, who was only about twenty years old, became well known as a religious mystic. She lived in a one-room building that was attached to the local church. She had requested that the priest allow her to live out a life of prayer, writing, and counseling the people.

Julian observed mass by looking through a window that opened into the interior of the church. Individuals needing spiritual strength would come to the window of her room for advice and comfort. She penned very comforting words for them—words that did not rely on the standard religious language of the day. They presented hope and cheer in a day when the church preached fear and punishment. The community came to see her as a steadying influence during such upheaval and death all around them. Julian became their spiritual counselor.

Julian left her indelible mark even from a life of simplicity and solitude. Her most famous line, written in the time of a horrible pandemic surrounded by death, offered hope with her words of comfort.

I will close with the truth she spoke so long ago:

> *All shall be well, and all shall be well,*
> *and all manner of thing shall be well.*
> Julian of Norwich (1330 CE)

ACKNOWLEDGEMENTS

A book requires a network to help it become a reality. Many thanks to my first editor Cynthia Furlong-Reynolds who started me on the journey of discovering what it takes to actually produce the book that was in my head. Mission Point Press under the leadership of Doug Weaver and Anne Stanton put together a team to improve and publish my work. That team included Tanya Muzumdar my editor, Darlene Short, Angela Saxon, the artist who designed the beautiful cover and text, Hart Cauchy, the social media consultant and Noah Shaw, the website designer.

Thanks to Russ Carney who was first to suggest that I write a book about what I was sharing in a class at St. Peter Lutheran Church. To Ron Cordell, author, professor and cousin who has always encouraged me and who inspires me with his free spirit and inquiring mind. To Mira Ptacin, my real live wildly successful island woman and author friend who offered me helpful tips on the entire process from writing to publishing. And most of all to Melinda Adams, my partner, best friend and lover who also served as my family editor and patient spouse during long hours of my absence in my writing den while working on the manuscript.

RESOURCE LIST

Books

Batchelor, Stephen. *After Buddhism: Rethinking the Dharma for a Secular Age*. New Haven, CT: Yale University Press, 2015.

Berry, Wendell. *Our Only World: Ten Essays*. Berkeley, CA: Counterpoint, 2015.

Bowen, Sarah. *Spiritual Rebel: A Positively Addictive Guide to Finding Deeper Perspectives and Higher Purpose*. Rhinebeck, NY: Monkfish Books, 2019.

Brooks, Arthur C. *Love Your Enemies: How Decent People Can Save America from the Culture of Contempt*. New York: Broadside Books, 2019.

Brooks, David. *The Second Mountain: The Quest for a Moral Life*. New York: Random House, 2019.

Bucko, Adam, and Matthew Fox. *Occupy Spirituality: A Radical Vision for a New Generation*. Berkeley, CA: North Atlantic Books, 2013.

Burton, Tara Isabella. *Strange Rites: New Religions for a Godless World*. New York: Public Affairs, 2020.

Eck, Diana L. *India: A Sacred Geography*. New York: Harmony Books, 2012.

Egan, Timothy. *A Pilgrimage to Eternity: From Canterbury to Rome in Search of a Faith*. New York: Viking, 2019.

Hadot, Pierre. *Philosophy as a Way of Life: Spiritual Exercises from Socrates to Foucault*. Oxford, UK: Blackwell Publishing, 1995.

Hamilton, Diane Musho. *Compassionate Conversations: How to Speak and Listen from the Heart*. Boulder, CO: Shambhala, 2020.

Harris, Sam. *Waking Up: A Guide to Spirituality Without Religion.* New York: Simon & Schuster, 2014.

Johnston, William, ed. *The Cloud of Unknowing and the Book of Privy Counseling.* New York: Doubleday, 1973.

Klein, Naomi. *On Fire: The (Burning) Case for the Green New Deal.* New York: Simon & Schuster, 2019.

Knitter, Paul F. *Without Buddha I Could not be a Christian.* London: Oneworld Books, 2009.

McIntosh, Steve. *Developmental Politics: How America Can Grow Into a Better Version of Itself.* St. Paul, MN: Paragon House, 2020.

McIntosh, Steve. *The Presence of the Infinite: T he Spiritual Experience of Beauty, Truth, and Goodness.* Wheaton, IL: Quest, 2015.

Moore, Thomas. *A Religion of One's Own: A Guide to Creating a Personal Spirituality in a Secular World.* New York: Penguin Books, 2014.

Pagels, Elaine. *Why Religion?: A Personal Story.* New York: Ecco, an Imprint of Harper Collins, 2018.

Perry, Kady. *New Orleans: Murals, Street Art & Graffiti, Volume 1.* Independent publisher, 2019. See #nolaartwalk on Instagram.

Pinker, Steven. *Enlightenment Now: The Case for Reason, Science, Humanism, and Progress.* New York: Penguin Books, 2018.

Ptacin, Mira. *Poor Your Soul.* New York: Soho Press, 2016.

Schildkret, Day. *Morning Altars: A 7-Step Practice to Nourish Your Spirit through Nature, Art, and Ritual.* Woodstock, VT: The Countryman Press, 2018.

Sheldrake, Philip. *Spirituality: A Very Short Introduction.* Oxford, UK: Oxford University Press, 2012.

Smith, Maggie. *Keep Moving: Notes on Loss, Creativity, and Change.* New York: Atria/One Signal Publishers, 2020.

Solomon, Robert C. *Spirituality for the Skeptic: The Thoughtful Love of Life.* Oxford, UK: Oxford University Press, 2002.

Tarnas, Richard. *The Passion of the Western Mind: Understanding the Ideas That Have Shaped Our World View.* New York: Harmony Books, 1991.

Tollifson, Joan. *Death: The End of Self-Improvement.* Salisbury, UK: New Sarum Press, 2019.

Podcasts

The Daily Evolver with Jeff Salzman

The Liturgists, Mike McHargue

NPR, All Things Considered, "Christians turn to podcasts to say things they can't say in church," March 5, 2020.

Revisionist History, Malcolm Gladwell explores life issues

YouTube and Other Media

The Common Heart—Spiritual Paradigm Shift, Rabbi Chava Bahle, TEDx Traverse City

Daniel Bonevac lectures on Philosophy

The Social Dilemma, a documentary that explores technology's influence on our lives

Websites and Email Letters

BrainPickings.org, a weekly online selection of great writings from the world's literature by Maria Popova

csh.umn.edu, University of Minnesota, Center for Spirituality and Healing

CulturalEvolution.org, the Institute for Cultural Evolution

DailyEvolver.com, by Jeff Salzman

DailyOM.com, by Madisyn Taylor

Headspace.com

Integrallife.com

Lonerwolf.com

Patheos.com, Article by Mark Feldmeir, "5 Ways to Find Common Ground this Election Season," September 15, 2020

SoundsTrue.com

Wildchurchnetwork.com

Made in the USA
Middletown, DE
10 July 2022

68977801R00099